Get ready for this work not only to form your mind, but also to touch your heart and soul. I'm afraid we Catholics take our sacramental life for granted. If you want a booster shot for a faith in the sacraments that has become a bit listless, keep on reading. Thanks, Msgr. Vaghi, for calling us back to the roots of our Catholic religion, the seven sacraments. You indeed proclaim the mysteries of our faith.

Most Reverend Timothy M. Dolan
Archbishop of New York

Msgr. Vaghi speaks out of his long pastoral experience in a way that helps the reader recognize that what is taking place in the sacramental sign is real. A delight to read and a joy to recommend.

Most Reverend Donald W. Wuerl
Archbishop of Washington

Msgr. Peter Vaghi's clear account of the seven sacraments is doctrinally sound, pastorally perceptive, and spiritually insightful. All who read this book will come to a greater appreciation of the *Catechism of the Catholic Church,* and so deepen their faith in Jesus and their love of the sacraments he instituted.

Thomas G. Weinandy, O.F.M. Cap.
Executive Director for the Secretariat for Doctrine
United States Conference of Catholic Bishops

What a treasure! Filled with reverence; careful research, and well-rounded, thoughtful questions—who could ask for more? Msgr. Peter Vaghi has done a great service for catechetical leaders looking for a summary of the seven sacraments of the Catholic Church that is practical and pastoral. This volume is a valuable resource for anyone who wants to understand these mysteries more deeply.

Carole Obrokta
Director of Religious Education
Archdiocese of New Orleans

This book shows that the sacraments are truly a celebration, a celebration of Christ's love as real as the love he showed when he walked the earth. Prepare yourself for a breath of fresh spiritual air—the heart and beauty of encountering Christ in the sacraments comes alive in these pages.

Carl A. Anderson
Supreme Knight
Knights of Columbus

the SACRAMENTS

we CELEBRATE

A Catholic Guide
to the Seven Mysteries of Faith

PETER J. VAGHI

foreword by
Archbishop Timothy M. Dolan

ave maria press AmP notre dame, indiana

Nihil Obstat: Reverend Michael Heintz, Ph.D.
            Censor Librorum
Imprimatur: Most Reverend John M. D'Arcy
            Bishop of Fort Wayne–South Bend
Given at Fort Wayne, Indiana, on October 15, 2009

© 2010 by Peter J. Vaghi

Founded in 1865, Ave Maria Press is a ministry of the Indiana Province of Holy Cross.

www.avemariapress.com

ISBN-10 1-59471-231-X   ISBN-13 978-1-59471-231-9

Cover image © JI Unlimited.

Cover and text design by David R. Scholtes.

Printed and bound in the United States of America.

Library of Congress Cataloging-in-Publication Data is available.

Dedicated to my three brothers, my two sisters-in-law, and my six nieces and nephews, whose continued encouragement and love have supported my priesthood in these twenty-five years.

Special gratitude to members of Little Flower Parish and the John Carroll Society; to my editor, Robert Hamma, to Gerald O'Collins, S.J., Father George Stuart, Adoreen McCormick, Monsignor William Millea, and Jeanmarie Keeney.

CONTENTS

Foreword

Alll the *invisible* realities of our redemption become *visible* in the sacraments," taught Pope Leo the Great sixteen centuries ago.

If you have trouble understanding just what Pope Leo was talking about, have I got a book for you—this one!

It won't take you long to conclude that the author, Monsignor Peter J. Vaghi, is a *parish* priest. He has spent the best part of more than two decades as a priest administering the sacraments. He has baptized hundreds of babies, heard thousands of confessions, celebrated Mass daily, married countless couples, and anointed thousands of infirm and elderly. In other words, he's been on the front lines of the battle for souls, armed with water, bread, wine, oil stock, purple stole, words, and gesture. His eloquent catechesis on the sacraments comes from his own deep priestly faith in their power and from years of pastoral experience.

But you'll also detect here the hand not of just a practitioner, but of a scholar. Monsignor Vaghi takes theology very seriously, so these chapters are laced with references to the *Catechism of the Catholic Church*, the documents of Vatican II, the magisterium of the Church—especially that of John Paul II and Benedict XVI, the Fathers of the Church, and an array of theologians.

That's why this book will be most beneficial for personal study, classroom work, adult faith-formation, and RCIA classes.

But get ready for this work to not only form your mind, but also to touch your heart and soul. I'm afraid we Catholics take our sacramental life for granted. If you want a booster shot for a faith in the sacraments that has become a bit listless, keep on reading.

Recently I welcomed back to Church a couple who sadly had left us a year or so ago to join an evangelical mega-church. I asked them what brought them back home. "We missed the sacraments," they answered. They must have read this book!

I especially welcome Monsignor Vaghi's book during this Year for Priests. I remember asking Father Callahan, my pastor growing up, what priests do all day. "Why, Tim, we administer the sacraments," he replied. That's the "stuff" of the priesthood. Just ask St. John Vianney, the Pastor of Ars and the patron saint of priests, who spent forty years in his tiny parish christening, celebrating Mass, marrying, anointing the sick, and hearing confessions. So effective was he that, as the historians record, before long, all of France was coming to Ars on their knees.

Thanks, Monsignor Vaghi, for calling us back to the roots of our Catholic religion, the seven sacraments. You indeed proclaim the mysteries of our faith.

Most Reverend Timothy M. Dolan
Archbishop of New York

Preface

In anticipation of my visit to a parish youth retreat, the pastor had led the group through the Way of the Cross—the Stations. For some, it was a first-time experience. One of the young people explained to me that he had often seen the pictures on the walls of the church but never knew the story behind them.

Much of our Catholic faith is expressed, celebrated, and lived through symbols and signs, some of them with the actual power to make present what they signify—to realize the story behind the symbol. That is what sacraments are—efficacious signs of grace instituted by Christ and entrusted to the Church by which divine life is dispensed to us.

Monsignor Peter Vaghi speaks out of his long pastoral experience in a way that helps the reader recognize that what is taking place in the sacramental sign is real. What I think readers will find most attractive about this work is the blending of theological content, pastoral insight, and an inviting style of writing.

This text provides anyone who wants to know more about the sacraments with a faithful summary of what the Church believes. It does so through the eyes of a pastor, communicating this wondrous mystery to busy people today who look for a deeper understanding of the faith that corresponds to their experience of life and their own yearning for a fuller and richer relationship with God. This book is a delight to read and a joy to recommend.

Most Reverend Donald W. Wuerl
Archbishop of Washington

Introduction

This is the second book in a series that looks at the four pillars of the *Catechism of the Catholic Church*: The Profession of Faith, The Celebration of the Christian Mysteries, Life in Christ, and Christian Prayer. The first book, *The Faith We Profess: A Catholic Guide to the Apostles' Creed*, examined the twelve articles of the Apostles' Creed. In this second volume, we reflect together on the sacraments.

We begin with an exploration of the sacraments as transforming encounters with Christ. At the outset, our focus is on the sacraments of initiation: Baptism, Confirmation, and the Eucharist (with two chapters devoted to this "sacrament of sacraments"). Next, our attention turns to the two sacraments of healing: Penance and Anointing of the Sick. We will conclude with a look at what the Catechism calls "sacraments at the service of communion": Holy Orders and Matrimony.

After each chapter there are a number of reflection questions and a prayer. These resources enable a small group to gather to reflect together on their faith. The prayer provided, or any familiar prayer, hymn, or psalm can be used to open and/or conclude each gathering. Of course, these resources can also be used personally to reflect and pray as one proceeds through this process.

The nine chapters will look at the sacraments and will draw from the great tradition of our Catholic faith as expressed in the universal *Catechism of the Catholic Church* (CCC). Our look at these mysteries will be enriched by references to the recently published *United*

States Catholic Catechism for Adults (*USCCA*). We will also examine the sacraments through the prism of the writings of our late Holy Father, John Paul II; Pope Benedict XVI; and the documents of the Second Vatican Council.

ONE

Sacraments: Transforming Encounters with Christ

How appropriate that the Church made "faith" the first pillar of the *Catechism of the Catholic Church*. For the Catechism is a book about faith, our faith—the faith of our mothers and fathers. It is a faith that, whether we consciously admit it or not, has sustained us throughout our lives—at moments of new life and at death, at times when we struggle to find meaning in otherwise meaningless situations, at those times of lifelong vocational commitments (be they marriage, consecrated life, vowed or ordained ministry), and all those many moments in between.

Our faith acts, often without our knowing it, as a lens through which we see the world, embrace the world, critique the world, and make efforts to live in a world that can be very challenging. And the Catechism is about faith. It is about faith seeking understanding, the mustering of reasons for our hope (cf. 1 Pet 3:15). It is about recouping a sense of joy in being a Catholic Christian. In faith, there are concrete answers to so many of our problems and challenges. Contemporary life need not simply be a continued and endless barrage of unanswered questions or open-ended confusion.

Christ, after all, is the answer, "the way, the truth, and the life." And the Catechism helps us understand

3

how it is that Jesus Christ is the answer to the human riddle. It helps us see this truth in a systematic and accessible way. The Catechism is a fundamental and organic synthesis of our entire faith, of what we believe as Catholics. In the words of John Paul II, it is "a sure norm for teaching the faith." We continually rejoice—or we should continually rejoice—in the great and mighty deeds God has done in order to save us. That is at the heart of our faith.

How is the Catechism arranged? There are four pillars (or four sections):

1. The Profession of Faith (what we believe, the creed)

2. The Celebration of the Christian Mystery (the sacraments, communal prayer, liturgy)

3. Life in Christ (the commandments, how we live, morality)

4. Christian Prayer (how we pray together and alone)

This pattern—creed, sacraments, morality, and prayer—followed the same format as the Roman Catechism that was published in the late sixteenth century after the Council of Trent. Although following the traditional order, the contents of both catechisms are often expressed in a new way in order to respond to the questions of our age and our American culture. Our precious faith is always old and always new.

Although developed in four parts, the Catechism manifests an interconnectedness among the parts, an organic structure to the presentation of the faith. Unity is, after all, an essential feature of the Christian faith.

Faith must be seen in its totality, not in selected reflections simply on parts that we find congenial, a kind of "a la carte" Catholicism. The Catechism seeks to build a synthesis, an organic view of the faith. This is its special strength.

In this book—the eight chapters that follow—we will look at the second section of the Catechism, a section titled "The Celebration of the Christian Mystery." The corresponding section in the *United States Catholic Catechism for Adults* is titled "The Sacraments: The Faith Celebrated." Both catechisms treat the sacramental and liturgical life of the Church. They explain how God's salvation, accomplished once and for all through Jesus Christ in the Holy Spirit, is made present and prolonged in time and space, in our time and space. It happens in the sacred actions of the Church's liturgy, especially in the seven sacraments. Both catechisms explain how the liturgy and the sacraments of the Church enable each one of us to become a real part in God's plan to save the world, to draw life from the risen Lord with each and every sacramental encounter, a life that continues to transform and change us and make us concrete icons of the Lord Jesus for the world to see. The teaching we will study is concrete and not just theoretical. Hopefully, it will answer or at least raise questions that you might have.

Today's Challenges

Now in my twenty-fifth year of priesthood, I have come to appreciate more and more the statement of the Catechism that "the sacred liturgy [itself] does not exhaust the entire activity of the Church: it must be preceded by evangelization, faith and conversion" (CCC 1072). So many of our Catholic people fail to understand the rich and life-giving meaning of the sacraments, of the Church's liturgy—often through no fault of their own. All the more do we have reason to reflect prayerfully on the sacraments: the sacraments as a whole and the seven individual sacraments. The Catechism is a very helpful way to make that study. It is a wonderful gift of the Church.

The following challenges, however, underscore some areas of much-needed attention. They come from my own pastoral experience.

I will always remember a couple whom I helped prepare for marriage shortly after I was ordained. In our first session, before talking about the sacrament of Marriage, I asked them what I thought would be a fundamental and basic question—what is a sacrament? Surprisingly, and to my chagrin, the best answer I could get was: "A sacrament is a gift of God." When I said that good weather was also a gift of God, I was met by blank stares. Together they could name only four of the seven sacraments. They both had gone to Catholic grade schools, high schools, and even excellent Catholic colleges. I know that, regrettably, this experience of mine is symbolic of a wider phenomenon in the Church, then and now. What is most problematic is that the seven sacraments are distinctively fundamental to the Church that Christ founded. In fact, their celebration helps define us as Catholics.

As Gerald O'Collins and Mario Farrugia stated succinctly:

> They [the sacraments] are seven privileged means that have been entrusted to his

Church by Christ and make his saving work
personally present for men and women until
the end of time. These sacraments are both
perceptible signs (which can be seen, heard,
tasted, touched, and smelled), central means
for the common worship of God, and special
vehicles of grace provided by the glorified
Christ. They confer and strengthen the life of
grace in the particular form that each sacrament symbolizes.

We cannot be discouraged, however, by recent polls
about the number of Catholics who attend Mass each
Sunday. Some polls have said that only 25 to 30 percent
do so. Citing the Code of Canon Law, the Catechism
states that "the Church obliges the faithful to take part
in the Divine Liturgy on Sunday and feast days" (CCC
1389). Our challenge is always to encourage our friends
and family members to come with us to Sunday Mass
and to be with us when our parish family gathers each
week.

Nor can we ignore the reality that the celebration of
the sacrament of Penance has dropped off considerably
in the Church since the Second Vatican Council. There
are hopeful signs of a renewed interest in this marvel-
ous healing sacrament. By way of example, "The Light
Is On for You" Lenten outreach in the Archdiocese of
Washington and the perennial "Come Home for Christmas" outreach in many parishes around the country
have borne fruit.

Also, there are those who fail to consider, before receiving Holy Communion, whether they are worthy to
receive the Body and Blood of Jesus Christ, and whether
they should first receive the sacrament of Penance. The

Catechism teaches that "anyone conscious of a grave sin must receive the sacrament of Reconciliation before coming to communion" (*CCC* 1385).

Many Catholics in their twenties and thirties have not received the sacrament of Confirmation. The Catechism clearly teaches that "Confirmation is necessary for the completion of baptismal grace" (*CCC* 1285). Together, Baptism, Confirmation, and the Eucharist constitute the "sacraments of Christian initiation." Since the three form a unity, without Confirmation and the Eucharist, Baptism is certainly valid and efficacious, but Christian initiation remains incomplete. Along with Confirmation and Holy Orders, Baptism imprints an "indelible character" on the soul of the recipient.

It is often unknown that the Anointing of the Sick (what used to be called Extreme Unction or the last rites) "is not a sacrament for those only who are at the point of death" (*CCC* 1514). It is available for those who are seriously sick, elderly, or facing a serious operation.

Parents sometimes delay having a child baptized, using the so-called argument that they will wait to allow the child to decide which faith he or she chooses to have. They have brought a child into the world. Surely they should also bring their child into the family of God. The Catechism states: "The Church and the parents would deny a child the priceless grace of becoming a child of God were they not to confer Baptism shortly after birth" (*CCC* 1250).

Not all have learned, moreover, the definition of a sacrament from childhood: "A sacrament is an outward sign instituted by Christ to give grace." Or as the Catechism states: "The sacraments are efficacious signs of grace, instituted by Christ and entrusted to the Church, by which divine life is dispensed to us" (*CCC* 1131). I would suggest that you commit either definition to memory if you do not already know it. This is the only formula that I will ask you to memorize in this entire book.

The Celebration of the Paschal Mystery

In the pages ahead I will emphasize the special aspects of each of the individual sacraments. In this introduction, I wish to highlight what is common to all of the sacraments—a celebration of the Paschal mystery of Christ, of his dying and rising and our encounter with him in each of the sacraments, each bringing with it "some particular grace" (*USCCA* 169).

To understand the concept of sacrament, it is important to understand its biblical roots. The word *sacrament*, or the Latin word *sacramentum*, was first used by Tertullian, a Christian writer who lived in Africa around AD 200. It is the Latin translation of the Greek word *mysterion*. This word *mysterion* gives us a significant key to the richness of the sacramental and liturgical life. Commonly translated, it means "mystery." It is not a mystery in the sense of an Agatha Christie novel with complicated plots or clever ploys.

St. Paul uses the word *mysterion* twenty-one times. From it the Latin word *sacramentum* derives. In Ephesians 3:9, he writes of the "plan of the mystery hidden for ages in God." In Ephesians 5:32, referring to marriage, he calls it "a great mystery."

The word *mystery* means the "work of God."

> The wonderful works of God among the people of the Old Testament were but a prelude to the work of Christ the Lord in redeeming mankind and giving perfect glory to God. He accomplished this work principally by the Paschal mystery of his blessed Passion, Resurrection from the dead, and glorious Ascension, whereby "dying he destroyed our death, rising he restored our life." . . . The Church celebrates in the liturgy above all the Paschal mystery by which Christ accomplished the work of our salvation. (CCC 1067)

This Paschal mystery—this dying and rising—is a mystery because it is the action of God. It is a mystery gradually unveiled and revealed in Christ Jesus. This mystery is unveiled to those who have been called to and initiated in the faith—you and me. For those outside the faith, it is still a mystery.

The liturgy, the sacramental life of the Church, puts us in touch with and lets us share in the hidden, inner (mysterious) life of God, revealed in the words and deeds of Jesus, most fully in the Paschal or Easter mystery—his death and Resurrection. Liturgy, from the Greek *leitourgia,* means "public work." In our context, it means our participation in the work of God—principally in our celebration of his Paschal mystery. Liturgy is the work of the entire Trinity. "At every liturgy, the action of worship is directed to the Father, from whom all blessings come, through the Son in the unity of the Holy Spirit" (*USCCA* 167). Although the entire body of Christ celebrates the liturgy, within the assembly, the ordained person has a unique function of service (*USCCA* 171).

It would be a mistake to consider the seven sacraments, those primary liturgical moments in our lives as Catholics, as isolated events with no link to each other or no link to Christ and his Church. They are various aspects of the one Paschal or Easter mystery. Each in their own way, they prolong in time and space the unique mystery of Jesus Christ, above all his passion, death, and Resurrection—out of love for us. Through the liturgy, through the sacraments, Christ himself, along with all he did to save us, is rendered present.

Each sacramental encounter brings us in touch with the living and risen Jesus Christ, an encounter that changes and transforms us, that is, gives us grace. It is God's unique vehicle for reaching and changing you and me. The Catechism emphasizes that "for believers" the sacraments are "necessary for salvation" (*CCC* 1129). At the same time, even though God works primarily through the sacraments, "he also touches us through the community of the Church, through the lives of holy people, through prayer, spirituality and acts of love" (*USCCA* 170).

> Christian liturgy not only recalls the events that saved us but also actualizes them and makes them present. The Paschal mystery of Christ is celebrated, not repeated. It is the celebrations that are repeated, and in each celebration there is an outpouring of the Holy Spirit that makes the unique mystery present. (*CCC* 1104)

"He did this once for all when he offered up himself" (Heb 7:27).

The whole liturgical life of the Church revolves around the Eucharistic sacrifice of the Mass and the other sacraments. "Sacraments are 'powers that come forth' from the Body of Christ, which is ever-living and life-giving. They are the actions of the Holy Spirit at work in his Body, the Church. They are 'the masterworks of God' in the new and everlasting covenant" (*CCC* 1116).

In Pope Benedict's book, *Jesus of Nazareth*, he asks a perceptive question at the outset: What did Jesus actually bring us? He states: "The answer is very simple: God." At the end of the book, he states that "man needs one thing." He states: "He needs God." In the sacraments, each of us encounters God. We uniquely encounter the transforming power of Jesus, the Son of God.

To this end, I invite you to contemplate the beautiful fresco at the beginning of this section of the Catechism. The early Christian depiction of the woman suffering from a hemorrhage, who is healed by contact with Jesus' robe, serves to symbolize the sacramental life of the Church. To understand this passage more fully, remember that a person with a hemorrhage was considered unclean, separated from the faith. By her healing, she became clean and reunited to the faith. So too, the sacraments heal, cleanse, and unite us to the Body of Christ. They continue in our day the works that Christ had performed during his early life. The sacraments are, as it were, "powers that go forth" from the Body of Christ to heal the wounds of sin and to give us the new life of Christ. "Jesus' words and actions during his hidden life and public ministry were already salvific, for they anticipated the power of his Paschal mystery" (*CCC* 1115). The sacraments uniquely bring us God and the divine power.

In this chapter, I will review the seven sacraments from a very specific angle. Later chapters will expand our understanding of the individual sacraments. Hopefully, they will help us see how each sacrament brings us in touch with the living and risen Jesus, the Jesus who died and rose out of love for us. Hopefully, we will understand more deeply how each one of the sacraments brings us, even now in our day, into the dying and rising experience, the Paschal event accomplished by Jesus out of love for us and our salvation. The sacraments are transforming encounters. They are not isolated events. They are a part of one central mystery, *mysterion*, his Easter mystery.

> The Paschal mystery of Christ . . . cannot remain only in the past, because by his death he destroyed death, and all that Christ is— all that he did and suffered for all men— participates in the divine eternity, and so transcends all times while being made present in them all. The event of the Cross and Resurrection *abides* and draws everything toward life. (CCC 1085)

Each sacrament is our transformative share in the dying/rising experience of Jesus, which is essential for our salvation.

Baptism: "The person baptized belongs no longer to himself, but to him who died and rose for us" (CCC 1269). The baptized becomes forever a member of the living Body of the risen Christ.

Confirmation: The person receives the full outpouring of the Holy Spirit, the Holy Spirit who is the Easter gift given on Pentecost as recorded in the Acts of the Apostles (2:1–36).

Eucharist: It is the sacrament of sacraments, the memorial, the rendering present of the dying and rising of Christ, the sacrament that strengthens our union, our communion, with the risen Christ and each other. It is a growth in the grace of Baptism that makes possible growth in the Christian life.

Penance: It is a dying to sin and in the words of the Catechism "a true 'spiritual resurrection'" (CCC 1468). Why? It restores us to the life of the risen Lord by bringing death to sin, healing, and reconciliation.

Anointing: "By the grace of this sacrament the sick person receives the strength and the gift of uniting himself more closely to Christ's Passion: in a certain way he is consecrated to bear fruit by configuration to the Savior's redemptive Passion" (CCC 1521). In this sacred anointing, the gift of "peace" is received from the Holy Spirit. It gives the recipient the courage to overcome the difficulties of serious illness.

Holy Orders: The priest acts "in the person of Christ" as representative of Christ, head of the Church. He is a vessel for Christ. Christ acts through the person of the priest. The priest is configured to Christ by a special grace of the Holy Spirit, the Easter gift, to serve as Christ. "The ordained priesthood guarantees that it really is Christ who acts in the sacraments through the Holy Spirit for the Church" (CCC 1120).

Marriage: Christ enters a special covenant with a man and woman who become a married couple. "Christ dwells with them, gives them the strength to take up their crosses and so follow him, to rise again after they have fallen, to forgive one another, to bear one another's burdens" (*CCC* 1642). This encounter with Christ enables couples to give to each other the same kind of total, free, and selfless love that characterized Christ's love on the Cross for us, a deep share in his Paschal mystery. Referring to marriage as the great mystery, *mysterion*, St. Paul compares it, the love between a man and woman, to that loving relation of Christ and the Church (Eph 5:32).

Each of these sacraments has consequences for the Christian life. Each one shapes how we lead our lives as followers of Jesus. "The saving grace of the dying and rising of Christ are communicated to us in the Sacraments so that we might live more perfectly Christ's truth and virtues such as love, justice, mercy, and compassion" (*USCCA* 176).

I encourage you to read a part or all of a chapter each day and make it a part of your daily prayer. Use the Scripture references as you read. Please do not become discouraged. Our faith is not simply formulas in a catechism but rather the realities they express. Our trust in the reality of God does not end with the formal or material expression of doctrine. It leads us to the personal reality of God proclaimed by that doctrine. At the heart of this treatment of the sacraments is the mystery of a living person, the mystery of Jesus Christ. That is the challenge of the Catechism: to let God help us to touch him. He continues to reveal himself to each of us in beautiful ways. In the words of Pope Benedict, Jesus came to bring us God.

Reflect

1. How does your faith serve as a lens through which you see the world? How would your perspective be different if you lacked the gift of faith?

2. How have you experienced the Paschal mystery—dying and rising with Christ—in your own life?

3. Reflect on and share a sacramental moment when you experienced the presence of Christ in a personal way.

Pray

Paul's Prayer

Blessed be the God and Father of our Lord
    Jesus Christ,
who has blessed us in Christ with every
    spiritual blessing in the heavens,
as he chose us in him, before the foundation
    of the world,
to be holy and without blemish before him.
For this reason I kneel before the Father,
from whom every family in heaven and on
    earth is named,
that he may grant you in accord with the
    riches of his glory
to be strengthened with power through his
    Spirit in the inner self,

and that Christ may dwell in your hearts
through faith;
that you, rooted and grounded in love,
may have strength to comprehend with all
the holy ones
what is the breadth and length and height
and depth,
and to know the love of Christ that surpass-
es knowledge,
so that you may be filled with all the fullness of God.
Now to him who is able to accomplish far
more than all we ask or imagine, by the
power at work within us,
to him be glory in the church
and in Christ Jesus to all generations, forever and ever. Amen.

—Ephesians 1:3–4, 3:15–21

TWO

Baptism: Gateway to the Christian Life

T he first residential Archbishop of Washington, Cardinal Patrick O'Boyle, was once asked the question: "What was the most important day of your life?" One would have thought that his answer would have been the day he was ordained a priest, or perhaps more obviously the day he became a cardinal. But his answer was immediate and clear: "The day of my Baptism."

There is much wisdom in that response. The challenge of this chapter, as we study this first of the three sacraments of initiation, is to help make the response of Cardinal O'Boyle credible and understandable.

Jesus' Baptism and Our Own

As if to underscore the importance of Baptism as well, Benedict XVI's first chapter in his book, *Jesus of Nazareth*, is titled "The Baptism of Jesus." In the waters of the Jordan he inaugurates his public ministry by being baptized by his precursor and cousin, John the Baptist. The pope writes:

> Jesus' Baptism anticipated his death on the Cross, and the heavenly voice proclaimed an

anticipation of the Resurrection. These anticipations have now become reality. John's baptism with water has received its full meaning through the Baptism of Jesus' own life and death. To accept the invitation to be baptized now means to go to the place of Jesus' Baptism. It is to go where he identifies himself with us and to receive our identification with him. The point where he anticipates death has now become the point where we anticipate rising again with him.

So important was Baptism for Jesus that his final words in Matthew's gospel, his mission statement to his disciples, was, "Go therefore and make disciples of all nations, baptizing them in the name of the Father and of the Son and of the Holy Spirit" (Mt 28:19). Referring to these words, Pope Benedict writes: "The Baptism that Jesus' disciples have been administering since he spoke those words is an entrance into the master's own Baptism—into the reality that he anticipated by means of it. That is the way to become a Christian."

Before looking specifically at the sacrament of Baptism, it is important to understand that the sacraments, each instituted by Christ himself, touch the various stages and important moments of the Christian life. The *Catechism of the Catholic Church* teaches that the sacraments "give birth and increase healing and mission to the Christian's life of faith. There is thus a certain resemblance between the stages of natural life and the stages of the spiritual life" (*CCC* 1210).

The Gateway to the Christian Life

As I have mentioned in the Introduction, it would be a mistake to consider the seven sacraments as merely isolated events with no link to each other or to Christ and his Church. They are various aspects of the one Paschal or Easter mystery—various aspects of one mystery. Each in their own way prolongs in time and space that unique mystery of Jesus Christ. Each sacramental encounter brings us in touch with the living and risen Jesus Christ, an encounter that changes and transforms us and gives us grace.

Baptism, that most important day in a Christian's life, is the gateway to the sacramental life in the Church. The Catechism calls it "the basis of the whole Christian life" (CCC 1213). "The person baptized belongs no longer to himself, but to him who died and rose for us" (CCC 1269). The baptized becomes forever a member of the living body of the risen Christ. As Pope Benedict writes about Baptism: "It is to go where he identifies himself with us and to receive our identification with him. The point where he anticipates death has now become the point where we anticipate rising again with him."

Baptism is thus the first of three sacraments of initiation. The others are Holy Eucharist and Confirmation. Baptism was not just an event when one was a child (for most of us), or later for some, an occasion for a family party or a one-day celebration. It is also importantly the opportunity to be cleansed of original sin, that sin of Adam inherited by each of us. Baptism is so much more. Baptism is a lifetime challenge. And Baptism is a daily challenge. It calls us to live out those promises we made (or our sponsor made for us) on the day of our

Baptism—the rejection of sin and the profession of our Catholic faith.

But what makes it possible for us to live out these promises? What happens at Baptism that makes it so important? There is an amazing thing that happens. In Baptism, God puts his very life in us. Baptism comes from the Greek word *baptizo,* which means "to plunge or immerse." Baptism plunges us into the very life of God. "It is no longer I who live, but Christ who lives in me" (Gal 2:20). The baptized have "put on Christ" (Gal 3:27). Baptism is birth into the new life of Christ. It is the beginning of our walk with the Lord.

St. Paul spells it out even more beautifully in the Letter to the Romans. Baptism expresses our sharing in Christ's dying, burial, and Resurrection to new life. "Do you not know that all of us who have been baptized into Christ Jesus were baptized into his death? We were buried therefore with him by baptism into death, so that as Christ was raised from the dead by the glory of the Father, we too might walk in newness of life" (Rom 6:3–4).

And this "newness of life" has real consequences. We become new creatures. We put on Christ. With such assurance, each of us may wonder about sharing this new life with others. Recall the famous question of the Ethiopian eunuch to the apostle Philip in the Acts of the Apostles. As they were traveling in the chariot and they came upon some water, the eunuch said, "Look, there is water. What is to prevent my being baptized?" (Acts 8:36). How many of our friends and family members might just need a nudge to bring them to the waters of Baptism? They might just wonder what is to prevent them from being baptized. The greatest hidden secret of our Church is the large number of newly baptized Catholics who enter the Church at the Easter Vigil each year after months of preparation through the Rite of Christian Initiation of Adults. The challenge belongs to each of us who are baptized to witness daily that newness of life in our homes and in our workplaces. No one should remain forever without an answer to the Ethiopian eunuch's question of what is to prevent one from being baptized. The answer belongs to each of us.

The *United States Catholic Catechism for Adults* (184–187) helps us understand the consequences of Baptism by looking at the eight major elements of the baptismal liturgy itself. After all, each sacrament teaches through its symbolic elements. Each sacrament accomplishes what it signifies.

The Rite of Baptism

The Sign of the Cross: At the beginning of the ceremony, the sign of the cross is made on the forehead of the person to be baptized, symbolizing Christ's saving death. Baptism is a sacrament of salvation.

Readings from Scripture: Through the readings, the Holy Spirit sheds light on the celebration and increases the faith of the participants with the light of revealed truth.

Exorcism and Anointing: Baptism liberates us from sin, both original and personal, and all punishment due to sin. With the oil of salvation, the person to be baptized is called to renounce sin and leave behind the power of evil.

Blessing of the Baptismal Water: This prayer asks that the Holy Spirit may be sent upon the water and that the baptized may be "born of water and the Holy Spirit."

Renunciation of Sin and Profession of Faith: Sin is rejected and faith professed either by the person to be baptized or by the sponsor (in the case of babies). Baptism is the sacrament of faith. It is the sacramental entry into the life of Christian faith.

The Essential Rite: Water is poured three times, or the person is immersed three times, with the words: "I baptize you in the name of the Father, and of the Son, and of the Holy Spirit." In Baptism, we become reborn as children of God the Father forever; we become united to Christ and his whole Body, the Church; and we become temples of the Holy Spirit. Plunged into the water, we are immersed in the life of the Trinity, the life of God, who is Father, Son, and Holy Spirit. Water, the principal sign of Baptism, symbolizes so well what has happened. Water both destroys and gives life. Prefigured in the Old Testament, especially in the crossing of the Red Sea, water expresses liberation and freedom, as well as death or destruction to sin. Now in Baptism, it symbolizes birth to new life in the power of the Holy Spirit. Sins are buried and washed away as we die with Jesus and rise with him from immersion in the water or from being cleansed by the pouring of water.

Anointing with Sacred Chrism: Through this anointing, the baptized is forever incorporated into Christ, who was "anointed" priest, prophet, and king.

White Garment and Candle: These symbolize that the baptized is now clothed in the protective love of Christ and enlightened by him. The baptismal candle is lit from

the Easter candle, a sign of the Resurrection and a guide
for the pilgrimage of life.

Having listed these eight elements of the rite, I invite you to listen to St. Gregory of Nazianzus and his
beautiful description of Baptism:

> Baptism is God's most beautiful and magnif-
> icent gift. . . . We call it gift, grace, anointing,
> enlightenment, garment of immortality, bath
> of rebirth, seal, and most precious gift. It is
> called *gift* because it is conferred on those
> who bring nothing of their own; *grace* since
> it is given even to the guilty; *Baptism* because
> sin is buried in the water; *anointing* for it
> is priestly and royal as are those who are
> anointed; *enlightenment* because it radiates
> light; *clothing* since it veils our shame; *bath*
> because it washes; and *seal* as it is our guard
> and the sign of God's Lordship. (CCC 1216)

The Necessity of Baptism

Baptism is necessary for salvation. Jesus tells Nico-
demus: "Amen, amen, I say to you, no one can enter
the Kingdom of God without being born of water and
the Holy Spirit" (Jn 3:5). In Mark's gospel, Jesus, sending forth his disciples, commands them to baptize all
nations and says further: "Whoever believes and is
baptized will be saved" (Mk 16:16). Moreover, the Catechism makes it clear: "Baptism is necessary for salvation for those to whom the Gospel has been proclaimed
and who have had the possibility of asking for the sacrament. . . . *God has bound salvation to the sacrament of*

Baptism, but he himself is not bound by the sacraments" (*CCC* 1257).

But note well the Catechism also states: "Those who die for the faith, those who are catechumens, and all those who, without knowing of the Church but acting under the inspiration of grace, seek God sincerely and strive to fulfill his will, are saved even if they have not been baptized" (*CCC* 1281). God and his divine grace are not bound or limited by the sacraments.

The Catechism contains a whole section on the Baptism of infants. It describes infant Baptism as an "immemorial" tradition of the Church. Sometimes people wait many, many months for the right godparents to come, perhaps from a distance. That is not a good practice, nor is it the intention of the Church. The Church intends for a child to be baptized shortly after birth. Entry into Christian life gives access, albeit in a mysterious way, to true freedom and spiritual enrichment. This should not be denied, even to infants.

A word on selecting godparents is also in order here. Being a godparent is a very solemn responsibility. It is not enough to pick someone simply for personal, family, or even business reasons. If the parents are unable to rear the child as a good and devout Catholic, it is the responsibility of the godparents to do so. Much care should be taken in this choice.

Baptismal preparation is also a significant opportunity for the parents and godparents to renew their understanding of the faith and the beautiful and profound understanding of the sacrament of Baptism itself. As a parish priest, I have so often experienced some beautiful moments of conversion in the lives of parents and godparents precisely during the preparation class for

Baptism. It becomes a unique opportunity to reflect on our precious Catholic faith, perhaps in a group, as they hold an infant in their arms during this time of preparation before the sacrament is celebrated.

Often when we speak of heaven, hell, and purgatory, we speak of limbo. It traditionally has been seen as the fate after death of infants who (obviously through no fault of their own) were not baptized. The theory of limbo has attempted to deal with the situation of the souls of infants who die subject to original sin and without Baptism. Thus they neither merit the beatific vision, "the contemplation of God in his heavenly glory" (CCC 1028), nor are subjected to any punishment because they are not guilty of any personal sin. Limbo was proposed as a state where unbaptized infants spend a happy eternity, but without communion with God.

On January 19, 2007, the International Theological Commission issued its study on the "theory" of limbo. It held that this theory, not even mentioned in the Catechism because it has no clear foundation in revelation, reflects "an unduly restrictive view of salvation." Because of original sin, Baptism is certainly the ordinary way to salvation, and parents are urged to baptize their children as soon as they can. At the same time, the commission concluded that there are reasons for prayerful hope that unbaptized infants who die will be saved and enjoy the beatific vision. The Church's hope for these infants' salvation reflects a growing awareness of God's boundless love and mercy. "Allow us to hope that there is a way of salvation for children who have died without Baptism" (CCC 1261). But the Catechism quickly adds: "All the more urgent is the Church's call not to prevent little children coming to Christ through the gift of holy Baptism" (CCC 1261).

So important is Baptism that Jesus began his own public ministry only after first being baptized himself by John the Baptist in the Jordan. In fact, the *United States Catholic Catechism for Adults* teaches: "The origin and foundation of Christian Baptism is Jesus" (184). In the words of St. Gregory of Nazianzus, "He comes to sanctify the Jordan for our sake and in readiness for us; he who is spirit and flesh comes to begin a new creation through the Spirit and water." Jesus' baptism at the Jordan is a manifestation of his own self-emptying, a self-emptying that is made more explicit on the Cross, out of love for each of us. In fact the blood and water that flowed from his side on the Cross (cf. Jn 19:34) symbolize Baptism and the Eucharist. St. Ambrose of Milan writes: "See where you are baptized, see where Baptism comes from, if not from the Cross of Christ, from his death. There is the whole mystery: he died for you. In him you are redeemed, in him you are saved" (CCC 1225).

And after his Resurrection, Jesus gives his mission to his apostles: "Go therefore and make disciples of all nations, baptizing them in the name of the Father and of the Son and of the Holy Spirit, teaching them to observe all that I have commanded you" (Mt 28:19–20). Yes, Baptism is necessary for salvation, as is the Church herself, which we enter by Baptism.

The Effects of Baptism

Our call to holiness is also rooted in Baptism. At that time of the liturgical year when we celebrate the Solemnity of All Saints, we focus on the call to holiness, both those canonized saints and those men and women who live holy lives—each of us, we pray. This call, indeed this vocation, is rooted in Baptism, and it is a call for each of us to heed. St. Paul sets forth a practical plan for holiness, a plan made possible by the grace of our Baptism. He urges us to "put on, then, as God's chosen ones, holy and beloved, heartfelt compassion, humility, gentleness and patience, bearing with one another. If one has a grievance against another, as the Lord has forgiven you, so must you also do. And over all these put on love, that is, the bond of perfection" (Col 3:12–13). St. Paul never tires of urging us, each and every baptized Christian, to live "as is fitting among saints" (Eph 5:3).

I wrote earlier that the anointing with sacred chrism, during the baptismal rite, signifies that the newly baptized person is incorporated into Christ who himself was "anointed" priest, prophet, and king. In fact, that anointing was the basis of the mission of Christ as Savior, to be priest, prophet, and king.

In Baptism, the very mission of Jesus becomes our mission. By Baptism, we, too, become "anointed ones." Each of us becomes another Christ. The prayer during the anointing with chrism at the Baptism of adults expresses this:

> The God of Power and Father of our
>   Lord Jesus Christ
> has freed you from sin,
> and brought you to new life
> through water and the Holy Spirit.
> He now anoints you with the chrism of
>   salvation,
> so that, united with his people,

you may remain forever a member of
     Christ
who is Priest, Prophet, and King.

Baptism gives us an indelible spiritual sign, a character, which consecrates us to Christ forever. Given once, Baptism cannot be repeated nor lost.

But, what does it mean to share today in the mission of Jesus, who was priest, prophet, and king? In other words, what are the concrete implications, the challenges of Baptism in the life of a lay person today, in my life as a priest? How is it that a baptized lay person uniquely shares in Jesus' mission today?

First, what about the priestly mission of Jesus? Perhaps you have never considered how a lay person shares in the priestly mission of Jesus. You might have thought that this was reserved to the ordained clergy. But both the laity and the ordained share in the priestly mission of Jesus, though in different ways.

An ordained priest is most a priest when he offers the sacrifice of the Mass. After the model of Jesus the high priest, he offers the Eucharistic sacrifice, "a holy exchange of gifts." Simple ingredients of bread and wine are offered and become the Body and Blood of Christ. Our humble earthly offerings are transformed into Christ himself.

Each baptized person, by offering every part of his or her life to God, just as a priest offers the sacrifice of the Mass, also shares in the priesthood of Jesus Christ. That is made possible by the anointing of Baptism.

> The supreme and eternal Priest, Christ Jesus, since he wills to continue his witness and service also through the laity, vivifies them

in this Spirit and increasingly urges them on to every good and perfect work. For besides intimately linking them to His life and His mission, He also gives them a sharing in His priestly function of offering spiritual worship for the glory of God and the salvation of men. For this reason the laity, dedicated to Christ and anointed by the Holy Spirit, are marvelously called and wonderfully prepared so that ever more abundant fruits of the Spirit may be produced in them. For all their works, prayers and apostolic endeavors, their ordinary married and family life, their daily occupations, their physical and mental relaxation, if carried out in the Spirit, and even the hardships of life, if patiently borne—all these become "spiritual sacrifices acceptable to God through Jesus Christ" (1 Pet 2:5). Together with the offering of the Lord's body, they are most fittingly offered in the celebration of the Eucharist. Thus, as those everywhere who adore in holy activity, the laity consecrate the world itself to God. (*LG* 34)

Remember the morning offering prayer? When we do this and offer everything in sacrificial praise to the Lord each day, each and every moment of the day (even our sufferings) becomes transformed, and so do we— like the bread and wine become transformed into the Lord Jesus during the sacrifice of the Mass. In the Eucharist, we gather every dimension of our lives together and present them, as we present the bread and wine, as an offering to God.

Through these daily efforts, daily life is made holy, the invisible but ever-present God is pointed to, and others can recognize the witness of service and prayer. Baptism thus makes it possible in this way for us to share in Jesus' own priesthood. The priesthood of the laity differs both in degree and in essence from the priesthood of the ordained, yet both are ordered to each other.

Second, what about the prophetic mission of Jesus?

Being a prophet is not what you might think of at first—a seer with a crystal ball foretelling the future. Prophets deal with God's holy and living Word. To share in the prophetic mission of Jesus, made possible by our Baptism, means quite simply to fall in love with the living Word of God, to interiorize it, to let it change us daily, to proclaim it in word and deed, to translate God's holy Word into one's family and social life, in all our choices, in what we do and say.

That happens only if and when the Word of God becomes a regular part of our daily lives. Through the power of the Holy Spirit, the same Holy Spirit who inspired God's Word in the first place, Sacred Scripture takes on a vital sense in our lives. This is made possible by the grace of our Baptism.

One way that we can live the prophetic mission of our Baptism is by preparing more reflectively for Sunday Mass, perhaps by reading the Sunday Scriptures as part of our daily agenda. Little by little, God's Word helps us see the world through a Christian lens. Gradually our perspective begins to change, and we look at the world through our prophetic mission.

Finally, through Baptism we share in the kingly mission of Jesus. How does this happen?

This should not be understood in the sense of the power and prestige of a king or any political leader. Jesus was a servant king, the Good Shepherd. He inaugurated a completely different kind of kingdom—one without geographical bounds.

St. Paul says the kingdom of God exists where there is "justice, peace and joy in the Holy Spirit" (Rom 14:17). Concretely, the kingdom proclaimed by Christ is the life of the Beatitudes, the Magna Carta of the kingdom of God—poverty, meekness, acceptance of suffering and persecution, desire for justice, peace, and charity. The laity share in the kingly mission of Jesus, made possible by the anointing at Baptism, uniquely through the secular character of the lay vocation. When one focuses on what is unique about one's calling and how through that work one can foster the coming of the kingdom of God, that is a participation in the kingly mission of Jesus. That vocation includes the promoting of justice, peace, and joy. It takes place not primarily on the altars of our churches, but in workplaces and homes. There are many practical ways to promote justice and peace in one's daily surroundings. In that way one lives out the kingly mission made possible by Baptism.

Always remember the day of your Baptism. Cardinal O'Boyle got it right. It is the most important day of our lives. It made us marked men and women for Jesus forever. It changed us and continues to change us, to infuse the life of God within us. It challenges us each day concretely to promote the threefold mission of Jesus as priest, prophet, and king. We pray that the blessings of our Baptism will grow deeper in us each and every day and that others will recognize us as Christians by what we say and do.

Reflect

1. When did you last attend a Baptism? What aspects of the celebration did you focus on? What new perspectives have you gained through this chapter?

2. How have you experienced water as a symbol of death? Of life? In what ways does water speak to you of the dying and rising of Christ?

3. How would you describe your vocation? What is God calling you to do?

Pray

A Morning Offering Prayer

Eternal Father, I offer you everything I do
  this day:
my work, my prayers, my apostolic efforts;
my time with family and friends; my hours
  of relaxation;
my difficulties, problems, distress, which I
  shall try to bear with patience.
Join these, my gifts, to the unique offering
which Jesus Christ, Your Son, renews today
  in the Eucharist.
Grant, I pray, that, vivified by the Holy
  Spirit
and united to the Sacred Heart of Jesus
and the Immaculate Heart of Mary,

my life this day may be of service to you
  and your children
and help consecrate the world to you.
  Amen.

—Apostleship of Prayer

THREE

Confirmation: Be Sealed with the Gift of the Holy Spirit

As we continue our journey through the sacramental way of life, we turn to the mystery and beauty of Confirmation. The Catechism is quite specific at the beginning of its rather brief section on this sacrament when it states that "the reception of the sacrament of Confirmation is necessary for the completion of baptismal grace" (CCC 1285). Baptism is the most important day of our lives as Christians. But if Confirmation is necessary for the completion of baptismal grace, then it, too, must be a part of that most important day, even if it takes place on another day.

One of the great joys of being in a parish with a school and a vibrant religious education program is the annual preparation for the sacrament of Confirmation. In our local church, this takes place in the eighth grade. Throughout the year as pastor, I assist with their retreat, give a series of meditations for their parents, and examine the candidates on their understanding of the sacrament. This includes conversations about the Confirmation name they have chosen and a discussion of their service hours—how they witness their faith before receiving the sacrament. It is always interesting to get to know our young candidates as they grow in faith and preparation for this great sacrament in which the bishop seals them with the gift of the Holy Spirit, and they pledge themselves to be stronger witnesses to our precious faith. Gerald O'Collins and Mario Farrugia write: "This sacrament constitutes in the Western Church a rite of passage for young adults who were baptized when they were babies. Confirmation comes at a time when they are expected to show themselves more mature and courageous witnesses." In the past, when one was confirmed, the term "soldier of Christ" was often used. It was both an expectation and a most descriptive name.

One of the Sacraments of Initiation

An importance aspect of this sacrament, and the young people consistently get this, is that Baptism, Confirmation, and the Eucharist together constitute the sacraments of Christian initiation. In other words, one becomes a full member of the Catholic Church only after reception of all three of these sacraments—sacraments that initiate a believer fully into the Catholic Church. Each of us is reborn in Baptism, strengthened by the Holy Spirit in Confirmation, and sustained each time we receive the Eucharist.

Important as it is to see these three sacraments together—a kind of sacramental triad—there exists an even more special relationship between Baptism, the first sacrament of initiation, and Confirmation. Confirmation completes the grace of Baptism. "By the sacrament of Confirmation [the baptized] are more perfectly bound to the Church and are enriched with a special strength of the Holy Spirit. Hence they are, as true witnesses of Christ, more strictly obliged to spread and defend the faith by word and deed" (*LG* 11*).* "The connection between Confirmation and Baptism is also reflected in the choosing of a name by which the candidate will be confirmed, especially when the chosen name is one of the names by which the candidate was baptized" (*USCCA* 206). For our young candidates, the invitation to choose a name from the vast array of holy men and women in our Christian tradition provides a unique opportunity to identify qualities of holiness they personally wish to emulate.

"A special strength of the Holy Spirit"—those are the operative words of this sacrament. Confirmation is about the full outpouring of the Holy Spirit, the Lord and Giver of life. Regrettably, the Holy Spirit, the third person of the Blessed Trinity, is sometimes referred to as the forgotten person of the Blessed Trinity.

The Sending of the Holy Spirit

The Old Testament prophets spoke of the Spirit. Referring to the long-awaited Messiah who would come to save the world, Isaiah announced: "The spirit of the Lord shall rest upon him, a spirit of wisdom and of understanding, a spirit of knowledge and of fear of the Lord" (Is 11:2).

Each of us has ingrained in our memory the beautiful image from the gospels of the dove, the sign of the Holy Spirit, hovering over Jesus as he is baptized in the Jordan by John—thus fulfilling the prophecy of Isaiah. Furthermore, "he was conceived of the Holy Spirit; his whole life and his whole mission are carried out in total communion with the Holy Spirit whom the Father gives him 'without measure'" (*CCC* 1286). In his book, *Jesus of Nazareth*, Benedict XVI quotes the biblical scholar Joachim Gnilka: "The image of the dove may be a reminiscence of what the creation account says about the Spirit brooding over the waters (Gen 1:2); the word *like* ('like a dove') suggests that it is 'a simile for something that ultimately cannot be described.'"

But the fullness of the Spirit was not to remain uniquely the possession of the Messiah. Repeatedly in Scripture Jesus promised to send the Holy Spirit upon those who followed him and ultimately upon us. "Whoever believes in me, as Scripture says: 'Rivers of living water will flow from within him'" (Jn 7:38). Jesus uses this vital image of water in reference to the Spirit. Using the word *drink* referring to the same Holy Spirit, Benedict XVI, in his encyclical on hope, writes: "This is how Christians addressed one another. By virtue of their Baptism they had been reborn, they had been given to drink of the same Spirit and they received the Body of the Lord together, alongside one another" (*SS* 4).

Of course, this is after the Holy Spirit had been sent, after Jesus was glorified (Jn 7:39). For at the Last Supper, Jesus told his disciples: "I tell you the truth, it is better for you that I go. For if I do not go, the Advocate will not come to you. But if I go, I will send him to you" (Jn 16:7). He was referring to the Holy Spirit, or the Advocate. That promise was ultimately fulfilled after his death and Resurrection in the sending of the Holy Spirit. Now Jesus had to leave before the Spirit could come. He had to suffer, die, and rise before the Spirit could come. And the Spirit is the new law of love. There is no way we could live the ten commandments, or the two great commandments of loving God and neighbor, or the new commandment of love without the Holy

Spirit within us. In fact, it was at Pentecost, when the law of love was infused in the hearts of his disciples. In Romans 5:5, St. Paul teaches us: "God's love has been poured into our hearts through the Holy Spirit who has been given to us."

There are two accounts of the descent of the Holy Spirit in the New Testament. In the Gospel of St. John (20:19–23) the Spirit comes on Easter Sunday night. The scene is the upper room where the disciples were locked together for fear of the Jews. John's account underscores that the dying and rising of Jesus and his sending of the Holy Spirit as he promised are parts of a whole. They are part of one mystery.

> Jesus said to them again: "Peace be with you. As the Father has sent me, so I send you." And when he had said this, he breathed on them and said to them: "Receive the Holy Spirit. Whose sins you forgive are forgiven them, and whose sins you retain are retained" (Jn 20:21–23).

When we think of the coming of the Holy Spirit, most of us think of the second account reported by Luke (Acts 2:1–13). According to Luke, the descent of the Holy Spirit took place fifty days after Easter. The disciples were all huddled together in fear behind locked doors. Then suddenly a wind roared through the house, filling every room. People from every known country of the world had gathered outside in Jerusalem for what was the Jewish feast of Pentecost. They heard this roaring wind. Then tongues of fire, representing the Holy Spirit, came down upon the apostles, filling them with the Holy Spirit and making it possible for them to be

understood in every language. Immediately, the apostles went out and began to preach the crucified and risen
Jesus. Filled with the Holy Spirit, the apostles began to
proclaim "the mighty works of God." They were filled
with boldness and courage, and three thousand people
were added that very day to their number. This is what
can happen when we really yield to the power of the
Holy Spirit. It can and does happen in our lives.

While the two accounts are different because they
were addressed to different audiences and at different
times, the mystery of the sending of the Holy Spirit, as
promised by Jesus, is the same. That is what happens at
Confirmation.

The sacrament of Confirmation is based on both biblical accounts. On the very day of Pentecost Peter said
to those gathered outside, "Repent and be baptized,
every one of you, in the name of Jesus Christ for the
forgiveness of your sins and you will receive the gift of
the Holy Spirit" (Acts 2:38). "Those who believed in the
apostolic preaching and were baptized received the gift
of the Holy Spirit in their turn" (CCC 1287). The Acts
of the Apostles, that beautiful and inspired diary of the
early church, is replete with examples of Peter, Paul,
John, and others conferring the Spirit by the "laying on
of hands." This gesture came to symbolize the coming
of the Holy Spirit. This account of St. Paul in Ephesus is
very instructive:

> While Apollos was in Corinth, Paul traveled
> through the interior of the country and came
> to Ephesus where he found some disciples.
> He said to them, "Did you receive the Holy
> Spirit when you became believers?" They
> answered him, "We have never even heard

that there is a Holy Spirit." He said, "How were you baptized?" They replied, "With the baptism of John." Paul then said, "John baptized with a baptism of repentance, telling the people to believe in the one who was to come after him, that is, in Jesus." When they heard this, they were baptized in the name of the Lord Jesus. And when Paul laid his hands on them, the Holy Spirit came upon them, and they spoke in tongues and prophesied. (Acts 19:1–6)

The sacrament of Confirmation "'in a certain way perpetuates the grace of Pentecost in the Church.' . . . Very early, the better to signify the gift of the Holy Spirit, an anointing with perfumed oil (chrism) was added to the laying on of hands. This anointing highlights the name 'Christian,' which means 'anointed' and derives from that of Christ himself whom God 'anointed with the Holy Spirit'" (CCC 1288–1289).

The Rite of Confirmation

Before we look at Confirmation in more detail, remember the general definition of a sacrament: "The sacraments are efficacious signs of grace, instituted by Christ and entrusted to the Church, by which divine life is dispensed to us" (CCC 1131). Underscore the word *signs*. What is the "sign" of Confirmation?

The sign of Confirmation is the imposition of hands and the anointing with chrism on the forehead. The bishop, who is the ordinary or normal minister of this sacrament, says, "Be sealed with the gift of the Holy

Spirit" as he anoints the forehead of each individual with oil. It signifies and imprints a "spiritual seal."

Oil is a sign of healing and strength. "Anointing, in Biblical and other ancient symbolism, is rich in meaning: oil is a sign of abundance and joy; it cleanses (anointing before and after a bath) and limbers (the anointing of athletes and wrestlers); oil is a sign of healing, since it is soothing to bruises and wounds; and it makes radiant with beauty, health and strength" (*CCC* 1293).

The Catechism continues: "Anointing with oil has all these meanings in the sacramental life. The pre-baptismal anointing with the oil of catechumens signifies cleansing and strengthening; the anointing of the sick expresses healing and comfort. The post-baptismal anointing with sacred chrism in Confirmation and ordination is the sign of consecration" (*CCC* 1294).

By this anointing, the confirmand receives an indelible "mark," the seal of the Holy Spirit. Baptism and Confirmation both impart a mark or "character." And just as we can be validly baptized only once, so, too, we can be validly confirmed only once. This character "is the sign that Jesus Christ has marked a Christian with the seal of his Spirit by clothing him [or her] with power from on high so that he [or she] may be his witness" (*CCC* 1304). "This seal of the Holy Spirit marks our total belonging to Christ, our enrollment in his service forever, as well as the promise of divine protection" (*CCC* 1296).

When administering Confirmation, the bishop extends his hands over those about to be confirmed and invokes the outpouring of the Holy Spirit. This gesture, since the time of the apostles, has signified the gift of the Holy Spirit. He invokes the seven gifts of the Holy Spirit:

wisdom, understanding, knowledge, fortitude, counsel, piety, and fear of the Lord. "When we are responsive to the grace of Confirmation and the seven gifts of the Holy Spirit, we begin to bear. . . the twelve fruits of the Holy Spirit: love, joy, peace, patience, kindness, goodness, generosity, gentleness, faithfulness, modesty, self-control, and chastity (cf. *CCC*, 1832; Gal 5:22)" (*USCCA* 209).

The age for Confirmation varies throughout the United States and around the world. In many dioceses, it is conferred at junior high school age. In others, it is later in high school. A few dioceses confirm infants at the time of their Baptism to emphasize the unity of these two sacraments of initiation. In the Eastern Rite, Confirmation is always administered immediately after Baptism and is followed by participation in the Eucharist. This tradition highlights the unity of all three sacraments of initiation.

Adults who were not confirmed in adolescence can be confirmed at any age. If you have not received the sacrament or know someone who has not, speak to your parish priest. Preparation for Confirmation includes a deepening study of the gift of faith itself. It should "aim at leading the Christian toward a more intimate union with Christ and a more lively familiarity with the Holy Spirit—his actions, his gifts and his biddings—in order to be more capable of assuming the apostolic responsibilities of Christian life" (*CCC* 1309).

The ordinary minister of Confirmation is the bishop. Bishops are, after all, the successors of the apostles, and they have received the fullness of the sacrament of Holy Orders. "The administration of this sacrament by them demonstrates clearly that its effect is to unite those who receive it more closely to the Church, to her apostolic origins, and to her mission of bearing witness to Christ" (*CCC* 1313).

We have said that Confirmation completes or ratifies the graces given in Baptism. The effect of the sacrament is the full outpouring of the Holy Spirit granted to the apostles on the day of Pentecost. At our Confirmation, the Holy Spirit comes with the special sacramental graces to enlighten our minds and strengthen our wills, so as to enable us to live up to our Christian commitments and be a courageous witness to Christ. But what kind of grace does one receive from this sacrament? What are the effects of the outpouring of the Holy Spirit, and how does the Holy Spirit increase and deepen the baptismal grace at Confirmation? There are five concrete effects (*CCC* 1302–1305).

The Effects of Confirmation

Confirmation deepens our identity as sons and daughters of God. The Catechism says that the Holy Spirit in the sacrament of Confirmation "roots us more deeply in the divine filiation which makes us cry 'Abba! Father!'" (*CCC* 1303). How does this happen? Concretely, it happens in our lives through prayer. It is, after all, the Holy Spirit who prays within us. Prayer is most essentially the work of the Holy Spirit. Pope John Paul II wrote in his encyclical on the Holy Spirit: "It is a beautiful and salutary thought that, wherever people are praying in the world, there the Holy Spirit is, the living breath of prayer" (*DV* 65).

It is important for us to recognize this truth. In addition, it is the Holy Spirit, the power of God, who draws us into divine life, into that unique relationship between the Father and the Son. In fact, St. Augustine describes the Holy Spirit as the love between the Father and the Son. The Holy Spirit is the energy of God, the grace of God moving us and pulling us into relationship with him. It is the Holy Spirit who reveals Jesus to us anew in our prayer. It is the Spirit who gives vitality to the words we read in Sacred Scripture, who unleashes the power of God pregnant in each and every word of Scripture—originally inspired by the same Holy Spirit in the sacred authors.

Confirmation forges a stronger union with Christ. With the outpouring of the Holy Spirit at Confirmation, each one of us benefits from the promise of the Lord Jesus who said: "And when he [the Holy Spirit] comes, he will convict the world in regard to sin" (Jn 16:8). Confirmation helps us strengthen our union with Christ because it gives us the grace to overcome sin. Any spirituality worth its salt has to deal with sin. Otherwise it is merely an illusion.

We can and should not be afraid to identify and deal with sin, the concrete patterns and indeed the structure it takes in our lives. Sin separates us from God and from the love that is God. It is precisely the Holy Spirit who reveals our sinfulness to us, and in the words of St. John "will convict the world in regard to sin" (16:8). The surest sign of the work of the Holy Spirit in our lives is that active struggle within each of us between the flesh, that drive toward selfishness and self-centeredness, and the Spirit. St. Paul stresses this:

> I say, then: live by the Spirit and you will certainly not gratify the desire of the flesh. For the flesh has desires against the Spirit, and the Spirit against the flesh; these are

opposed to each other, so that you may not do what you want. But if you are guided by the Spirit, you are not under the law. Now the works of the flesh are obvious: immorality, impurity, licentiousness, idolatry, sorcery, hatreds, rivalry, jealousy, outbursts of fury, acts of selfishness, dissensions, factions, occasions of envy, drinking bouts, orgies, and the like. I warn you, as I warned you before, that those who do such things will not inherit the kingdom of God. In contrast, the fruit of the Spirit is love, joy, peace, patience, kindness, generosity, faithfulness, gentleness, self-control. Against such there is no law. Now those who belong to Christ (Jesus) have crucified their flesh with its passions and desires. If we live in the Spirit, let us also follow the Spirit. Let us not be conceited, provoking one another, envious of one another."(Gal 5:16–26)

In his book on the Holy Spirit titled *The Life-Changer,* Father Francis Martin writes:

Do you ever feel like your life is a record, playing the same old songs over and over again? Sin has cut its own grooves in every one of us. We all have these patterns or structures of sin in our lives. They enslave us and those around us because, as we have seen, structures of sin involve our relationships with others. The plain fact is, however, that the Lord does want to change our lives and the lives of those with whom we live and have to do. Our acknowledgment and confession of sin need not be an embarrassing repetition in which we acknowledge, over and over, the same disordered habits and tendencies. No, the power of the Cross of Jesus Christ, uniting us with his body through Baptism, by a faith enlivened in the Holy Spirit, can actually change our lives. The power of the Cross can give us an inner, living experience of the presence and power of Christ within us. This becomes the source of our confidence, joy, freedom, and assurance in the Holy Spirit. Having that precious pledge of eternal salvation, we can know already in this life what it means to be free from those things which hold us in bondage. The Holy Spirit will show us the ways in which we habitually fall short of his glory.

Often it is during the sacrament of Penance itself that the Holy Spirit reveals our sinfulness. The Holy Spirit makes us see our sins so clearly and makes it possible for the burden of sin to be lifted and the mercy of God to be experienced anew or for the first time. That is the concrete experience of the effect of the Holy Spirit.

Confirmation increases the gifts of the Holy Spirit within us. Like the apostles on Pentecost, we, too, receive an outpouring of the Holy Spirit. When he confers Confirmation, the bishop prays over the candidates:

> Send your Holy Spirit upon them
> To be their Helper and Guide.
> Give them the spirit of wisdom and
> understanding,

> The spirit of right judgment and
>   courage,
> The spirit of knowledge and reverence.
> Fill them with the spirit of wonder and
>   awe in your presence.

The Catechism teaches that "the moral life of Christians is sustained by the gifts of the Holy Spirit. These are permanent dispositions which make us docile in following the promptings of the Holy Spirit" (CCC 1830). Spiritual writers have sometimes associated the seven gifts of the Holy Spirit with the three theological virtues of faith, hope, and charity, and the four cardinal virtues of prudence, justice, fortitude, and temperance.

Confirmation perfects our bond with the Church. The gifts of the Spirit are given to build up and strengthen the Church, the Body of Christ. In speaking of the gifts that we receive, St. Paul says:

> As a body is one, though it has many parts,
> and all the parts of the body, though many,
> are one body, so also Christ. For in one Spirit
> we were all baptized into one body, whether
> Jews or Greeks, slaves or free persons, and
> we were all given to drink of one Spirit.
> (1 Cor 12:12–13)

By completing Baptism, Confirmation deepens and perfects our bond with the Church.

Confirmation strengthens us. Confirmation importantly "gives us a special strength of the Holy Spirit to spread and defend the faith by word and action as true witnesses of Christ, to confess the name of Christ boldly, and never to be ashamed of the Cross" (CCC 1303). An essential fruit of the sacrament and the working of the Holy Spirit is to equip us for mission, the mission of evangelization in a countercultural way in this world. The task may seem daunting at times, but this is exactly why Christ himself strengthens us in the power of the Holy Spirit, so that we can truly say and understand from the core of our being that "I can do all things in Christ, who strengthens me" (Phil 4:13). Confirmation calls us not only to say this, but to do it by our very actions.

There are many examples that confirm that Pentecost is not just an event that happened in our Church centuries ago. You can list them in your own lives. There are many personal examples at home and work that daily testify that the fruits of Confirmation continue to happen each time a person is confirmed, each time one of us yields to and calls upon the power of the Holy Spirit abiding within us. For a Christian, Confirmation is his or her personal Pentecost.

In summary, "the effects of Confirmation include a permanent character, a perfection of baptismal grace, an increase in the gifts and fruits of the Holy Spirit, a deepening of our identity as adopted sons and daughters of God, a closer bond to the Church and her mission, and helps for bearing witness" (*USCCA* 210). Like the grace of Baptism, this sacrament is not magic. God gives us the grace. God gives us his Holy Spirit. It is up to us to respond. In the Prayer over the People, the bishop prays:

> God, complete the work you have begun
> and keep the gifts of your Holy Spirit active
> in the hearts of your people. Make us ready
> to live the gospel and eager to do your will.
> May we never be ashamed to proclaim to all

the world Jesus, who lives and reigns forever.
(Rite of Confirmation)

Reflect

1. What memories do you have of your
    Confirmation? What did Confirmation mean to
    you when you received it?

2. Has it been true in your life that the Holy Spirit
    is the forgotten person of the Blessed Trinity?
    Are there any occasions when you have prayed
    to the Holy Spirit? Has this chapter opened any
    new understandings of the role of the Spirit in
    your life?

3. Which of the seven gifts of the Holy Spirit is
    most operative in your life? Which gift do you
    most need to grow in?

4. Confirmation "gives us a special strength of
    the Holy Spirit to spread and defend the faith."
    How do you do that in your life?

Pray

Come, Holy Spirit, Creator blest,
and in our souls take up Thy rest;
come with Thy grace and heavenly aid
to fill the hearts which Thou hast made.
O comforter, to Thee we cry,
O heavenly gift of God Most High,
O font of life and fire of love,

and sweet anointing from above.
Thou in Thy sevenfold gifts are known;
Thou, finger of God's hand we own;
Thou, promise of the Father, Thou
Who dost the tongue with power imbue
Kindle our senses from above,
and make our hearts o'erflow with love;
with patience firm and virtue high
the weakness of our flesh supply.
Far from us drive the foe we dread,
and grant us Thy peace instead;
so shall we not, with Thee for guide,
turn from the path of life aside.
Oh, may Thy grace on us bestow
the Father and the Son to know;
and Thee, through endless times confessed,
of both the eternal Spirit blest.
Now to the Father and the Son,
Who rose from death, be glory given,
with Thou, O Holy Comforter,
henceforth by all in earth and heaven.
Amen.

—attributed to Rabanus Maurus (776–856)

FOUR

Eucharist:
The Sacrament of Love

The title of this chapter comes from Benedict XVI's first apostolic exhortation, *Sacramentum Caritatis* or *Sacrament of Love*. The subtitle is *On the Eucharist as the Source and Summit of the Church's Life and Mission*. It was issued on February 22, 2007, following the 2005 Roman Synod of Bishops on the Eucharist.

For me, one of the great privileges of being a pastor is the annual celebration of First Holy Communion and all the preparation that leads to that wonderful spring day. I always include in my homily to the children the beautiful, memorable, and instructive words of St. Thérèse of Lisieux (the patroness of our parish, Little Flower) about her First Holy Communion. In her *Story of a Soul*, she writes of her memory of that day as if it were yesterday:

> The "beautiful day of days" finally arrived. The *smallest details* of that heavenly day have left unspeakable memories in my soul! The joyous awakening at dawn, the *respectful* embraces of the teachers and our older companions! The large room filled with *snow-white* dresses in which each child was to be clothed in her turn! Above all, the procession

52

into the chapel and the singing of the *morning* hymn: "O altar of God, where the angels are hovering!"

I don't want to enter into detail here. There are certain things that lose their perfume as soon as they are exposed to the air; there are deep *spiritual thoughts* that cannot be expressed in human language without losing their intimate and heavenly meaning; they are similar to ". . . *the white stone I will give to him who conquers, with a name written on the stone which no one KNOWS except HIM who receives it.*"

Ah! How sweet was that first kiss of Jesus! It was a first kiss of *love*; I *felt* that *I was loved*, and I said, "I love You, and I give myself to You forever!" There were no demands made, no struggles, no sacrifices. . . .

What the Little Flower described as "that first kiss of Jesus," Pope Benedict XVI describes as "nuclear fission":

The substantial conversion of bread and wine into his body and blood introduces within creation the principle of a radical change, a sort of "nuclear fission," to use an image familiar to us today, which penetrates to the heart of all being, a change meant to set off a process which transforms reality, a process leading ultimately to the transfiguration of the entire world, to the point where God will be all in all (cf. 1 Cor 15:28). (*SC* 11)

The Eucharist is, moreover, (in the words of the Catechism) the "source and summit of the Christian life

. . . the sum and summary of our faith" (*CCC* 1324, 1327). It is not a footnote to the faith. In instituting the Eucharist on the night before he died, Jesus sought "to perpetuate the sacrifice of the cross throughout the ages until he should come again" (*CCC* 1323). In the words of Benedict XVI: "In the Eucharist Jesus does not give us a 'thing,' but himself; he offers his own body and pours out his own blood. He thus gives us the totality of his life and reveals the ultimate origin of this love" (*SC* 7). It is the sacrament of charity.

"In Memory of Me"

At the Last Supper, Jesus commanded his apostles: "Do this in memory of me." But what does this command mean? "Remembering," the living out that memory of what God has done for us on the Cross, is much more than the simple ability to recall it and recite it.

In the Eucharist, we remember then what Jesus did and continues to do out of love, how he suffered, died, rose, and sent his Holy Spirit for us. We celebrate and remember that supreme act of love of the God-man each and every time we gather for the Eucharist.

What we remember and celebrate is not just a "remembrance" in the common understanding of that word, for example, remembering a good novel or a good friend. It is so much more.

The supreme act of love in which Jesus died and rose is what we remember each time we celebrate the Eucharist. Moreover, it actually brings us into an intimacy with him at a most profound level at the very moment of reception. There is no better way to deepen our friendship, knowledge, and love of Jesus than the

Eucharist and to experience the depth of his love for us, of him who died that we might forever live with him.

The Eucharist also has "drawing" power. Pope Benedict beautifully and perceptively writes that in the Eucharist "we [actually] enter into the very dynamic of his self-giving" (*SC* 11). In the Eucharist, Christ's sacrifice on the Cross continues to impart in us the dynamism of His generous love. We become like Christ. Effectively, we become Eucharist for others.

An Inexhaustible Mystery

So rich and inexhaustible is this mystery, this sacrament, that the Catechism spells out the different names that have been used to describe it (cf. *CCC* 1329–32):

> *Eucharist*: Because it is an action of thanksgiving to God.
>
> *Eucharistein*: Because *Eucharist* means "to give thanks" in Greek.
>
> *The Lord's Supper*: Because of its connection with the supper that the Lord took with his disciples on the eve of his Passion, when he instituted this sacrament.
>
> *The Breaking of Bread*: Because by this action the disciples first recognized Jesus after the Resurrection (Lk 24:13–35).
>
> *Eucharistic Assembly*: Because the Eucharist is celebrated amidst the assembly of

the faithful, the visible expression of the Church.

The Memorial of the Lord's Passion and Resurrection.

The Holy Sacrifice of the Mass: Because it makes present the one sacrifice of Christ.

Divine Liturgy: Because the Church's whole liturgy finds its center and most intense expression in the celebration of this sacrament.

The Most Blessed Sacrament: Because it is the Sacrament of sacraments.

Holy Communion: Because by this sacrament we unite ourselves to Christ, who makes us sharers in his Body and Blood to form one single Body.

Holy Mass: The liturgy concludes with the sending forth of the faithful to fulfill their mission in the world. The word *Mass* comes from the Latin word for *sent, missio.*

At its heart, however, it is the sacrificial love of Jesus, his dying and rising for us that we celebrate in each and every Mass. Every Eucharist is this commemoration, this memorial (this making present of a past event), this reenactment of his death on Calvary and his glorious Resurrection, and this memorial of his wonderful love for us. It is love in its most radical form.

The Second Vatican Council twice referred to the Eucharist as the "source and summit" of our lives as Christians. The Catechism uses that same language. In fact, it is the subtitle of the apostolic exhortation issued by Benedict XVI , *Sacramentum Caritatis*. Two questions thus follow:

1. Why is the Eucharist the source of our lives as Christians?

2. Why is the Eucharist the summit of our lives as Christians?

The Source of Our Lives as Christians

> The Lord Jesus on the night in which he was betrayed took bread, and after he had given thanks, broke it and said, "This is my body, which is for you. Do this in remembrance of me." In the same way, after the supper, he took the cup, saying, "This cup is the new covenant in my blood. Do this, whenever you drink it, in remembrance of me." (1 Cor 11:23–25)

The bread we eat and the cup we drink is Jesus Christ. It is really Jesus. It is his real presence. It is not a figurative or metaphorical presence. It is always good to spend some time meditating and focusing on what happens at the Eucharist. It is, after all, the principal mystery of our Faith.

Faith in the real presence, I fear, has decreased in recent years. Note the lack of reverence in Church. The failure to genuflect and the talking in Church are reflective of this. The real presence needs to be spoken about more frequently—as a stimulus for the faith. Each of us should seek to grow in faith in the Eucharist. It takes faith to recognize Jesus in the breaking of the bread. It is a faith for which we should continually pray. It might help to kneel before the Blessed Sacrament and ask God to help our unbelief. A simple little prayer will do, such as: Jesus, strengthen my faith to believe in you more deeply in the Eucharist!

Regarding the real presence, the sixteenth-century Council of Trent teaches: "By the consecration of the bread and wine there takes place a change of the whole substance of the bread into the substance of the body of Christ our Lord and of the whole substance of the wine into the substance of his blood" (CCC 1376). In other words, the substance of bread and wine is completely annihilated; only the appearance of bread and wine remains. Jesus is really, truly, and substantially present under the appearance of bread and wine. "The mode of Christ's presence under the Eucharistic species is unique" (CCC 1374). "This presence is called 'real'—by which is not intended to exclude the other types of presence as if they could not be 'real' too, but because it is presence in the fullest sense: that is to say, it is a substantial presence by which Christ, God and Man, makes himself wholly and entirely present" (USCCA 223). "Christ is thus really and mysteriously made present" (CCC 1357). The Catholic Church has fittingly and properly called this change of substance "transubstantiation."

But what effect does transubstantiation have? Why is the Eucharist the source of our life?

Whoever shares in the Eucharist receives strength, nourishment, healing, consolation, encouragement to live as a true Christian. It is the very life of God within us. It is our source and the principal means to our growth in holiness.

Jesus' presence in the Eucharist is not a passive presence. It is active and dynamic. In the Eucharist, Jesus is attaching us to what he does in the Paschal mystery—his definitive victory over sin and death. He is attaching us to himself. In the Eucharist, we actually encounter the risen Jesus, a specific kind of encounter that transforms and changes us into him, the love that is his very person. So often we hear the axiom that we are what we eat or that we become that which we consume. In the Eucharist, we become like Jesus. "For my flesh is true food and my blood is true drink. Whoever eats my flesh and drinks my blood remains in me, and I in him" (Jn 6:55–56). What a compelling and indeed revolutionary promise from the revealed words of Jesus himself! "He who feeds on my flesh and drinks my blood has life eternal and I will raise him up on the last day" (Jn 6:54).

At the Twentieth World Youth Day in Germany, Pope Benedict XVI told the young people gathered from around the world on August 21, 2005: "The Body and Blood of Christ are given to us so that we ourselves will be transformed in our turn. We are to become the Body of Christ, his own Flesh and Blood. . . . He is within us, and we are in him. His dynamic enters into us and then seeks to spread outwards to others until it fills the world, so that his love can truly become the dominant measure of the world" (*USCCA* 227). The Eucharist is thus the Sacrament of Love.

In his book *Catholicism and Fundamentalism*, Karl Keating devotes two chapters to refuting, in a rather convincing way, the fundamentalist challenge that the language of Jesus in the Scripture regarding the "real presence" is simply symbolic or metaphorical. He draws our attention to the language of John 6. The early Christians had already experienced the tradition of the Eucharist for sixty years when this gospel was written around AD 90. This discourse on the bread of life is peculiar to St. John. Twelve times therein Jesus says he is the bread that came down from heaven; four times he says that they would have to "eat my body and drink my blood." The word for *eat* is used alongside the word *chew*, and thus this could not be a mere figurative presence.

And yet, even in Jesus' day, this was a hard teaching to accept. As we read the account in John 6:41–69, we notice first the "murmuring" among the Jews in protest when he claimed, "I am the bread that came down from heaven" (v 41). Then, the Jews quarreled among themselves saying, "How can he give us his flesh to eat?" (v 52). We learn that "from this time on, many of his disciples broke away and would not remain in his company any longer" (v 66). Finally, however, after the murmuring, the quarreling, the abandonment of some, Jesus says to the Twelve: "Do you want to leave me, too? Simon Peter answered him, 'Lord, to whom shall we go? You have the words of eternal life. We have come to believe; we are convinced that you are God's holy one'" (vv 67–69). Peter's confession of faith is a model for each of us. The very same challenge that is given to each of us was given to the first disciples. It must have been harder for them. Although they loved Jesus so much, they did not have our advantage: the knowledge that Jesus rose from the dead, the witness of the apostles after Pentecost in the power of the Holy Spirit, and two thousand years of living Tradition.

The Eucharist is a source of strength in this life now and a pledge of life eternal: "Whoever eats my flesh and drinks my blood has eternal life." Christ's sacrifice on the Cross imparts to us in the Eucharist the dynamism of his generous love.

"Holy Communion increases our union with Christ. 'Whoever eats my flesh and drinks my blood remains in me and I in him' (Jn 6:56). Communion with the Body of Christ preserves, increases, and renews the life of grace received at Baptism" (*USCCA* 224). It likewise "offers us strength, called grace, to preserve us from mortal sin. By deepening our friendship with Christ, this Sacrament makes it more difficult for us to break our union with him by mortal sin" (*USCCA* 225).

Yes, Jesus in the Eucharist is the source of our lives!

The Summit of Our Lives as Christians

When we come to the Eucharist on Sunday (the Lord's Day) or during the week as so many Catholics do regularly, we should be more conscious that, united with Christ, we bring with us all our prayers, works, sufferings, hardships, and joys. All are offered on the paten with the bread in worship to the Lord—everything that we are is raised to him as "summit." The Eucharist is the summit of our lives as Christians.

Lifted to God in perfect worship, our voices join with the angels and the saints. Not only is our praise carried to heaven, but we must be aware that wherever the Lord is, the angels are also present, worshiping and adoring him. We join with them as they are among us.

Through the action of the priest, the sacrifice of the Eucharist is united to the perfect sacrifice of Christ on the Cross. "The same Christ who offered himself once in a bloody manner on the altar of the Cross is contained and is offered in an unbloody manner" (CCC 1367). "Present and effective, Christ's sacrifice is applied to our lives. 'If the blood of goats . . . can sanctify those who are defiled how much more will the blood of Christ . . . cleanse our consciences from dead works to worship the living God' (Heb 9:14)" (USCCA 221).

"The sacrifice of Christ and the sacrifice of the Eucharist are *one single sacrifice*: 'The victim is one and the same: the same now offers through the ministry of priests, who then offered himself on the Cross; only the manner of offering is different'" (CCC 1367). The Eucharist is the sacrament of love in which Jesus died and rose and now lives forever with the Father. He is the Lamb on the throne who still bears the marks of slaughter and constantly intercedes for us.

The Eucharist is also the sacrifice of the entire Church.

> In the Eucharist the sacrifice of Christ becomes also the sacrifice of the members of his body [the Church]. The lives of the faithful, their praise, sufferings, prayer, and work, are united with those of Christ and with his total offering, and so acquire a new value. Christ's sacrifice present on the altar makes it possible for all generations of Christians to be united with his offering. (CCC 1368)

"The ordained priest in the Mass links the Eucharistic consecration to the sacrifice of the Cross and to the Last Supper, thus making it possible that the sacrifice of Christ becomes the sacrifice of all the members of the Church. . . . This also reminds us of the importance of sacrifice in each individual's life" (*USCCA* 221). The Eucharist is thus the summit of our lives as Christians.

The whole Church is united in love with the offering and intercession of Christ. "To the offering of Christ are united not only the members still here on earth, but also those already *in the glory of heaven*" (*CCC* 1370).

Yes, the whole Church, the pilgrim Church on earth and the Church in heaven, is united in the Eucharistic sacrifice. This has implications for us. When the bread and wine are transformed into the Body and Blood of the risen Jesus Christ at the moment of consecration, each one of us surrenders to him and becomes like him. We are brought into divine intimacy in a very special way. It is the culmination and summit of our spiritual lives.

"The cup of blessing which we bless, is it not a participation in the Blood of Christ? The bread which we break, is it not a participation in the Body of Christ?" (1 Cor 10:6). Could there be a more powerful contact with the Son of God than his own Body and Blood, the eating of his very Body and the drinking of his very Blood? What a profound mystery!

It is the sacrificial love of Jesus, his very self-gift, his dying and rising for us, that we celebrate at each and every Mass. Every Eucharist is the commemoration, the memorial (making present of a past event), the reenactment of his death on Calvary, and his glorious Resurrection, the memorial of his wonderful love for us.

The Church continually calls us to reflect on the central role of the Eucharist in Catholic life. If we are to face the great challenges of living the life of Christ and fulfilling his mission each day, we must appreciate ever anew the mystery that stands at the center of our Catholic faith and life, "its indispensable element." The Eucharist is thus the "source and summit" of our lives! How can we not resolve to come to know Jesus more deeply in the Eucharist and experience first-hand his saving and transforming love in this sacrament of love?

In conclusion, I cite Cardinal Angelo Comastri, who as Archbishop of Loreto a few years ago wrote for the Eucharistic Year an invitation for people to live the Eucharist, the sacrament of love, as a "gift of love." He wrote:

> Today, we are all asking ourselves what we can do to evangelize this deaf society which is apparently immunized against the Gospel. And what if we began believing more in the Eucharist? And what if we offered a show of unity and solidarity beginning from the Eucharist? I am sure that many people would begin to think and ask "Where do you find the strength to live like this?" And we would respond, "In the Eucharist!" and they would believe us. Yes, my dear friends, Love is contagious. So is the greatest gift on earth—the Most Holy and Blessed Eucharist!

Reflect

1. What memories do you have of your First Communion? What did Communion mean to you when you first received it?

2. Which of the names for this sacrament represents a new or unaccustomed way of thinking about it? What can you learn from thinking about the sacrament in this way?

3. What does the real presence of Jesus in the Eucharist mean to you?

4. How has this chapter enriched your understanding of the Mass as a sacrifice? What do you bring to this sacrifice?

Pray

Anima Christi

Soul of Christ, sanctify me.
Body of Christ, save me.
Blood of Christ, inebriate me.
Water from the side of Christ, wash me.
Passion of Christ, strengthen me.
O good Jesus, hear me.
Within your wounds conceal me.
Do not permit me to be parted from you.
From the evil foe protect me.
At the hour of my death call me.
And bid me come to you,
to praise you with all your saints
for ever and ever. Amen.

—Roman Missal

FIVE

Eucharist:
Ever Ancient, Ever New

"Behold, I stand at the door and knock. If anyone hears my voice and opens the door, I will enter his house and dine with him, and he with me" (Rev 3:20). As a loving friend, Jesus knocks at the door of our hearts and ardently desires to dine with us at the sacrificial meal we call the Eucharist.

How do we respond? Are we Sunday regulars? Weekday people? Irregular? Occasional?

Do we ever meditate on the fact that "as often as the sacrifice of the Cross . . . is celebrated on the altar, the work of our redemption is carried out" (CCC 1364)? It is awesome to think of the Eucharist in this way. How can we not celebrate the Eucharist if we understand that our very salvation, our redemption is at stake?

Do we hear the voice of Jesus calling us to dine with him? As we turn over in bed on Sunday morning, what do we do? What choice do we typically make and why? How can we refuse if we hear him, truly hear his voice?

Each of us needs to recoup in our day the unique and profound meaning of Sunday. Sunday is the day of the Lord, when the Eucharistic celebration becomes central to our lives. There is much competition for the Lord on Sunday. There is so much competition in our busy lives that keeps us even from getting the family together for an old-fashioned Sunday meal, that weekly gathering of relatives and friends to relax with each other and enjoy our family life together. Sunday Mass is the time the parish family comes together and praises the Lord. It is when we dress up and come to meet our God and do it together as a family.

The late Pope John Paul II once wrote that the Sunday Eucharist actually defines us as Catholics. In effect, it is a part of our spiritual DNA. Benedict XVI writes that "we need to remember that it is Sunday itself that is meant to be kept holy, lest it end up as a day 'empty of God'" (SC 73). The life of faith thus becomes endangered. "The celebration of the Christian Sunday remains . . . an indispensable element of our Christian identity" (DD 30) since it commemorates the radical newness brought and bought by Christ on that first day of the week—that first Easter. It distinguishes us as men and women of divine love in a profoundly renewed existence.

The Eucharist in God's Plan: A Marvelous History—Ever Ancient

"At the heart of the Eucharistic celebration are the bread and wine that, by the words of Christ and the invocation of the Holy Spirit, become Christ's Body and Blood" (CCC 1333).

Bread and wine! Think about them. Throughout all of salvation history, they appear over and over again, ultimately becoming in a surprising way the Body and Blood of Jesus Christ.

The Eucharist was prefigured in the Old Testament—the bread and wine offered by that mysterious king-priest Melchizedek; the manna in the desert by which God's chosen people were fed; the Passover meal that prefigured the Eucharist directly—the unleavened bread and the blessing cup.

Then there is the New Testament and the "multiplication of the loaves," an event found significantly in all four of the gospel texts. The Lord said the blessing, broke the bread, and gave it to the disciples to feed the multitude. Jesus' words and actions prefigure the Eucharist. Then there is the sign of water turned into wine at Cana—another image of the Eucharist and the second of the Luminous Mysteries of the rosary.

Now the actual institution itself!

> The Lord, having loved those who were his own, loved them to the end. Knowing that the hour had come to leave this world and return to the Father, in the course of a meal he washed their feet and gave them the commandment of love. In order to leave them a pledge of this love, in order never to depart from his own and to make them sharers in his Passover, he instituted the Eucharist as the memorial of his Death and Resurrection, and commanded his apostles to celebrate it until his return; "thereby he constituted them priests of the New Testament." (CCC 1337)

> "And he took bread, and when he had given thanks he broke it and gave it to them, saying, 'This is my body which is given for you. Do this in remembrance of me.' And likewise the cup after the supper, saying, 'This

cup which is poured out for you is the New
Covenant in my blood.'" (*CCC* 1339)

"Do this in memory of me." That was his command.
The three synoptic gospels (Matthew, Mark, and Luke
and St. Paul have handed on to us the account of the
institution. The fourth gospel does not include these
words of Eucharistic institution but has in their place
the foot washing—a symbolic way of giving expression
to the love that is the Eucharist itself. From the beginning, the Church has been faithful to the Lord's command, "Do this in memory of me."

What does the *do* mean in Christ's command? Surely
it is the breaking of the bread and the giving of the cup.
But it is so much more than that.

Theologian Raniero Cantalamessa, O.F.M. Cap., ex-
plains it this way: "He didn't in fact just mean: Do exactly
what I have done, repeat this same ritual. He was also
saying: Do the essence of what I have done, offer your
bodies as a sacrifice, as you have seen me do! For I have
given you an example, that you also should do as I have
done (Jn 13:15)." He says further, referring to Jesus' interior act that accompanies the action of the breaking of the
bread:

> Then I understand that to "do" what Jesus
> did that night, I must, first of all, "break" my-
> self and that is, lay before God all hardness,
> all rebellion towards him or towards others,
> crush my pride, submit and say "yes," fully,
> to all that God asks of me. I too must repeat
> the words: Lo, I have come to do thy will, O
> God! You don't want many things from me;
> you want me and I say "yes." To be Eucharist

like Jesus signifies being totally abandoned to the Father's will.

The Acts of the Apostles testifies that the Church has been faithful to the Lord's command from the very beginning. From the Church of Jerusalem, we read in Acts: "They devoted themselves to the apostles' teaching and fellowship, to the breaking of the bread and the prayers . . . Day by day, attending the temple together and breaking bread in their homes, they partook of food with glad and generous hearts (Acts 2:42, 46)" (CCC 1342).

The Acts further tells us that they gathered on "the first day of the week," the day of the Lord's Resurrection (Acts 20:7). Down to our own day, the same basic structure of the Eucharist has been used. Note the letter cited by the Catechism from St. Justin Martyr showing that as early as the second century, the basic lines for the order of the Eucharist were formed. St. Justin wrote to the pagan emperor Antoninus Pius (138–161) explaining what Christians did:

> On the day we call the day of the sun, all who dwell in the city or country gather in the same place.
>
> The memoirs of the apostles and the writings of the prophets are read, as much as time permits.
>
> When the reader has finished, he who presides over those gathered admonishes and challenges them to imitate these beautiful things.
>
> Then we all rise together and offer prayers for ourselves . . . and for all others, wherever they may be, so that we may be

found righteous by our life and actions, and faithful to the commandments, so as to obtain eternal salvation.

When the prayers are concluded, we exchange the kiss.

Then someone brings bread and a cup of water and wine mixed together to him who presides over the brethren.

He takes them and offers praise and glory to the Father of the universe, through the name of the Son and of the Holy Spirit and for a considerable time he gives thanks (in Greek: *eucharistian*) that we have been judged worthy of these gifts.

When he has concluded the prayers and thanksgiving, all present give voice to an acclamation by saying: "Amen."

When he who presides has given thanks and the people have responded, those whom we call deacons give those present "eucharisted" bread, wine and water and take them to those who are absent. (CCC 1345)

The Liturgical Celebration of the Eucharist—Ever New

There are two parts to every celebration of the Eucharist—the Liturgy of the Word and the Liturgy of the Eucharist. The Catechism is careful to point out, however, that "the liturgy of the Word and the liturgy of the Eucharist together form 'one single act of worship'" (CCC 1346).

One of my favorite passages in all of Scripture is Luke 24:13–35, the account of Jesus and two disciples on the road to Emmaus shortly after the Resurrection. If you study that story, you will see hidden therein a foreshadowing of these two parts of the Eucharist:

> *The Liturgy of the Word*: As Jesus walked along, he responded to their bewilderment, "Beginning with Moses and all the prophets, he interpreted to them what referred to him in all the scriptures."

> *The Liturgy of the Eucharist*: They did not recognize him as the Lord until he stayed with them after they reached their destination. "And it happened that, while he was with them at table, he took bread, said the blessing, broke it, and gave it to them. With that their eyes were opened and they recognized him. He was made known to them in the breaking of the bread."

To this day, the Eucharistic table set for us is the table of both the Word of God and the Body of the Lord.

Each time we all gather together for the Eucharist, it is Christ himself "who presides invisibly over every Eucharistic celebration" (*CCC* 1348). The priest represents Christ—*in persona Christi*. The priest presides over the assembly, speaks after the readings, receives the offering, and says the Eucharistic Prayer. But all have active parts to play in every Eucharist. Some are readers, some are extraordinary ministers of Holy Communion, some are in the offertory procession. But all are called to participate fully, actively, and consciously in the celebration of the Eucharist.

Focus now a little more closely on the Liturgy of the Word and the Liturgy of the Eucharist. The Liturgy of the Word includes the Scripture readings from the Old and the New Testament, the homily, the creed, and the general intercessions. The responsorial psalm is most often from the Book of Psalms—the prayer book of Jesus himself. Christ becomes present to us through the Scripture. He challenges us, critiques us, consoles us, affirms us, and in general speaks to us the Good News of his life, death, and Resurrection. In the homily, the priest or deacon breaks open the Word for us and exhorts us to accept the Word. The homily is followed on Sunday by the creed. Then the general intercessions are offered for the needs of the Church, society, and all the people.

The Liturgy of the Eucharist includes the preparation of the gifts (the offerings of bread and wine), the Eucharistic Prayer and the communion rite (the Lord's Prayer, sign of peace, Lamb of God, the breaking of the host and the reception of Holy Communion, and the closing prayer).

At the heart of the Liturgy of the Eucharist is the Eucharistic Prayer. It has several closely connected parts:

> *Thanksgiving* (expressed especially in the Preface): In this prayer, we thank God the Father, through Christ in the Spirit, for the gifts of creation, salvation, and sanctification.

> *Acclamation*: The whole congregation joins with the angels and saints in singing or saying the *Sanctus* (Holy, Holy).

Epiclesis (Invocation of the Holy Spirit): The Church implores the power of the Holy Spirit to change the bread and wine offered by human hands into Christ's Body and Blood.

Institution Narrative and Consecration: The priest proclaims Jesus' words at the Last Supper over the bread and wine. "The power of the words and the action of Christ, and the power of the Holy Spirit, make sacramentally present under the species of bread and wine, Christ's body and blood, his sacrifice offered on the Cross for all" (*CCC* 1353).

Anamnesis (Remembrance): We recall the death and Resurrection of Christ and look forward to his glorious return.

Second Epiclesis: The Holy Spirit is invoked upon the gathered community, to bring unity to the worshippers who will receive Holy Communion.

Intercessions: With the whole Communion of Saints and all God's people on earth, we pray for the needs of all the members of the Church, living and dead.

Doxology and Great Amen: We conclude the Eucharistic Prayer with praise of God the Father, through his Son Jesus Christ, in the Holy Spirit. This glorification is confirmed and concluded by the people's acclamation "Amen." (*USCCA* 219–220)

In the previous chapter, we looked at the Eucharist as the "source and summit" of our lives and the real presence of Jesus in the Eucharist. The real presence is the result of the words of the priest and the power of the Holy Spirit. Jesus is really, truly, and substantially present under the appearance of bread and wine. At the heart of the Church's teaching on the real presence is the understanding that the substance of bread and wine is completely annihilated; only the "appearance" of bread and wine remain. Note that this is different than saying that Jesus is really, truly, substantially present *in* the bread and wine.

The third part of the Liturgy of the Eucharist is the communion rite. It begins with the Our Father. The rite expresses both reconciliation (the sign of peace) and oneness and unity that result from each of us receiving the Body and Blood of Jesus. Receiving the Body and Blood of Jesus is not a private act. Unity with the Eucharistic Body of Christ brings communion (union with) within the Mystical Body. The Eucharist is a sign of Christian unity—the wafer of bread is one wafer from many grains and the cup of wine is pressed from many grapes. Each is in this way symbolic of Christ's Mystical Body, one body of many members, and of this body we are all an integral part.

Since the Second Vatican Council, emphasis has been placed on the Eucharist as *meal*. It is certainly that. It commemorates, after all, the Last Supper that was a meal. The Eucharist nourishes us with divine life as every meal nourishes us physically. But importantly, the Eucharist is also a *sacrifice*, for it represents in an unbloody manner Christ's sacrifice of love for us on Calvary.

The sacrifice of Christ and the sacrifice of the Eucharist are *one single sacrifice*. "The victim is one and the same: the same now offers through the ministry of priests, who then offered himself on the Cross; only the manner of offering is different. . . . And since in this divine sacrifice which is celebrated in the Mass, the same Christ who offered himself once in a bloody manner on the altar of the Cross is contained and offered in an unbloody manner . . . this sacrifice is truly propitiatory." (CCC 1367)

It is thus both meal and sacrifice. The altar, around which we gather, represents the two aspects of the same mystery: the altar of the sacrifice and the table of the Lord (CCC 1383). "The Mass is at the same time, and inseparably, the sacrificial memorial in which the sacrifice of the Cross is perpetuated and the sacred banquet of communion with the Lord's body and blood" (CCC 1382).

The Effects of the Eucharist

Above all, the Eucharist augments our union with Christ and our communion with each other (CCC 1391). "Whoever eats my flesh and drinks my blood remains in me and I in him. Just as the living Father sent me and I have life because of the Father, so also the one who feeds on me will have life because of me" (Jn 6:56–57).

At Mass, each of us meets Christ in a most special way. In faith, hope, and charity, the Christian receives the graces necessary for growth into an ever greater likeness of Christ. Holy Communion preserves, increases, and renews the life of grace received at Baptism. Through the graces of the Eucharist, we are enabled to relive the mysteries of Christ's life, death, and Resurrection in each of our own lives.

The Eucharist also strengthens our bonds of charity, and our love, especially for the poor (CCC 1397). One reason it is so important to recoup the sacrificial dimension of the Eucharist is to help us understand the fruits or consequences of the Eucharist. As is true with all sacraments, what it signifies is that which it brings about or effectuates. The breaking of the bread and the pouring of wine signify the breaking of Jesus' Body for us in sacrifice— all out of love for us. Every time we eat his Body and drink his Blood at Mass, we become love. The Eucharist brings about within us the love it signifies. This is an important consequence of understanding the Eucharist as sacrifice, a loving sacrifice of the Lord Jesus for each and every one of us. It is a consequence that moves and transforms us to live lives of charity.

The Eucharist separates us from sin, cleansing us from past sins and preserving us from future sins—especially mortal sins (CCC 1393, 1395).

The Eucharist makes the Church and the Church makes the Eucharist (CCC 1396). Those who receive the Eucharist are united more closely to Christ and through Christ to all the faithful into one body. This Body is the Church. "Communion renews, strengthens, and deepens this incorporation into the Church, already achieved by Baptism" (CCC 1396).

The Eucharist is a pledge even now of the glory that is to come (CCC 1402). Every time we celebrate the Eucharist, the work of our redemption is being carried out.

The Eucharist, in the words of St. Ignatius of Antioch, "provides the medicine of immortality, the antidote for death, and the food that makes us live forever in Jesus Christ" (CCC 1405).

In addition, Jesus quenches our hunger as he did for the crowds in the first part of John 6—the miracle of the multiplication of the loaves and fishes. That story is the only miracle story common to Matthew, Mark, Luke, and John—surely an image of the Eucharistic bread, "for the Jewish feast of the Passover was near." Even the language in John 6:11 recalls the institution of the Eucharist—"Jesus then took the loaves of bread, gave thanks [*eucharistein*] and passed them around."

Focus, if you will, on their hunger, on your hunger, and Jesus' response in a miraculous and mysterious way to the hunger of the "vast crowd," about five thousand. Jesus asked, "Where shall we buy bread for these people to eat?"

In the Eucharist, Jesus does not have to buy bread. Through the mysterious and sacramental action of the priest, Jesus becomes present on the altar. He addresses, however, the same kind of hunger in us that he did in the crowds of people assembled in John 6, a hunger for belonging, a hunger for healing and reconciliation, a hunger for growth in holiness. The Eucharist makes the Church and makes it possible for us to belong to Jesus, his living body, and to each other. The Eucharist heals—"Lord, I am not worthy to receive you, but only say the word and I shall be healed." In the Eucharist, we touch our God, we touch Jesus and, like the woman who was healed in the gospel by her touching the cloak of Jesus, so are we healed. Finally, our hunger for growth in holiness is met by Jesus in the Blessed Sacrament.

Yes, Jesus nourishes us, that deep hunger for God, a deep hunger satisfied by the Eucharist, the bread of life, the source of our life, this sacrament of love.

Our Preparation for the Eucharist

There seems to be a general feeling today that we have lost "the sense of the sacred" at Mass. One way to recoup that important sense is to prepare worthily for Mass. The *United States Catholic Catechism for Adults* is clear that we need to prepare for the invitation of Jesus to receive him in Holy Communion. It states: "The Church urges us to prepare conscientiously for this moment [reception of Holy Communion]. We should be in the state of grace, and if we are conscious of a grave or serious sin, we must receive the sacrament of Penance before receiving Holy Communion. We are also expected to fast from food or drink for at least one hour prior to the reception of Holy Communion" (*USCCA* 222).

The *Catechism of the Catholic Church* adds: "Bodily demeanor (gestures, clothing) ought to convey the respect, solemnity and joy of this moment when Christ becomes our guest" (*CCC* 1387).

St. Paul urges us to examine our conscience: "Whoever, therefore, eats the bread or drinks the cup of the Lord in an unworthy manner will be guilty of profaning the body and blood of the Lord" (1 Cor 11:27). "That means that all must examine their consciences as to their worthiness to receive the Body and Blood of our Lord. This examination includes fidelity to the moral teaching of the Church in personal and public life (United States Conference of Catholic Bishops, *Catholics in Political Life*, 2004)" (*USCCA* 222).

"The Church obliges the faithful to take part in the Divine Liturgy on Sundays and feast days and, prepared by the sacrament of Reconciliation, to receive the Eucharist at least once a year, if possible during the Easter season. But the Church strongly encourages the faithful to receive the holy Eucharist on Sundays and feast days, or more often still, even daily" (CCC 1389).

I wish to add a final word about Eucharistic Adoration outside of Mass as a wonderful means of preparation for Mass and for all the consequences that we pray result from a proper celebration of Mass itself. In his apostolic exhortation *Sacramentum Caritatis*, Benedict XVI wrote:

> The act of adoration outside Mass prolongs and intensifies all that takes place during the liturgical celebration itself. Indeed, "only in adoration can a profound and genuine reception mature. And it is precisely this personal encounter with the Lord that then strengthens the social mission contained in the Eucharist, which seeks to break down not only the walls that separate the Lord and ourselves, but also and especially the walls that separate us from one another."

When Jesus knocks, listen to him, follow him to the table at Mass or outside of Mass. In the Eucharist, He is "ever ancient and ever new." He alone provides "medicine for immortality."

Reflect

1. What does Sunday mean for you and your family?

2. "For I have given you an example, that you also should do as I have done" (Jn 13:15). How do you live Jesus' command, "Do this in memory of me," beyond the Mass?

3. What might you do to be better prepared for the celebration of the Sunday Eucharist?

4. How would you describe the difference the Eucharist makes in your life?

Pray

Ad Sacrosanctum Sacramentum

O sacred banquet at which Christ is
   consumed,
The memory of His Passion recalled,
our soul filled with grace,
and our pledge of future glory received:
How delightful, Lord, is Your spirit,
which shows Your sweetness to men,
offers the precious bread of heaven,
fills the hungry with good things,
and sends away empty the scornful rich.

V. You have given them bread from heaven.
R. A bread having all sweetness within it.

Let us pray:

God, Who left for us a memorial of your
Passion in this miraculous sacrament,
Grant we implore you, that we may
venerate the holy mystery of your Body
and Blood, so that we may ever experience in ourselves the fruitfulness of your
redemption, you who live and reign,
world without end. Amen.

—St. Thomas Aquinas

SIX

The Healing Sacrament
of Penance

It is not unusual to walk into a parish church anywhere in the world on a Sunday or Saturday vigil Mass and witness practically the entire congregation line up for Holy Communion. It is a beautiful sight to behold. In contrast, however, if you visit a parish church on Saturday afternoon or evening, or whenever the sacrament of Penance is being offered, you will typically notice a small line before the confessional. This phenomenon has seemingly occurred since the renewal of the Second Vatican Council. Yet, as Pope Benedict reminded us in his 2009 letter proclaiming the Year for Priests:

> In France, at the time of the Curé of Ars, confession was no more easy or frequent than in our own day, since the upheaval caused by the revolution had long inhibited the practice of religion. Yet he sought in every way, by his preaching and his powers of persuasion, to help his parishioners to rediscover the meaning and beauty of the sacrament of Penance. . . .

One can only ask what happened to diminish the frequent celebration of this wonderful healing sacrament, especially as a preparation for Holy Communion.

St. Paul clearly teaches: "Whoever, therefore, eats the bread or drinks the cup of the Lord in an unworthy manner will be guilty of profaning the body and blood of the Lord" (1 Cor 11:27).

We might ask whether we ever perceive ourselves as unworthy to receive the Body and Blood of Christ. Have we lost the sense of what worthiness means? Do we even know that we are required to receive Holy Communion worthily? Benedict XVI offers this perspective in his apostolic exhortation on the Eucharist: "We know that the faithful are surrounded by a culture that tends to eliminate the sense of sin and to promote a superficial approach that *overlooks* the need to be in a state of grace in order to approach sacramental communion worthily" (*SC* 20, emphasis added). Perhaps there is a bigger question: Have we lost the sense of sin—sin seen as burden, as a mystery, as darkness, even as a paralysis? Is sin even in our vocabularies?

Father John Baldovin, S.J., is quoted in *America* magazine: "On the one hand, we're not obsessed with sin any longer. On the other hand, people don't think of themselves as sinners, which is a big problem." In that same article, Archbishop Donald Wuerl concludes: "Many are not all that open to recognizing personal responsibility."

As a priest for almost twenty-five years, I have regularly promoted this wonderful sacrament (and made it a regular part of my life). I would suggest that emphasis must be placed on the healing nature of the sacrament. A friend suggested that sin is akin to plaque in one's arteries. Just as plaque inhibits the flow of blood, so also does sin inhibit our developing a relationship with God.

This sacrament of Penance is the healing antidote and treatment.

Happily, more and more efforts have been employed in recent years throughout our country to encourage a reawakening, or perhaps even an initial experience for many, of this healing sacrament. Negative statistics about the use of the sacrament are not an indication that there is no need for or value to this healing sacrament instituted by Christ. Outreach that encourages the celebration of the sacrament of Penance becomes an opportunity for genuine evangelization. In downtown Washington, for example, various parishes have funded for some time, with great success, a "Come Home for Christmas" campaign during Advent with creative posters in the Metro cars inviting people to come to confession before Christmas. The church names and confession times are listed. And happily, people come in great numbers. It is wonderful to experience, especially as a priest confessor, such a profound sense of repentance and joy. The Archbishop of Washington initiated a similar successful effort, with much advertising on buses and radios, an outreach titled "The Light Is On for You," inviting people to come to confession during Lent. The confession light is on during the same specific times weekly in every parish in the archdiocese. Other dioceses have made similar efforts to encourage reception of this wonderful healing sacrament and with great success. Generous priests and proactive laity helping to encourage more regular reception of this unique sacrament will continue to bear much fruit for our Church and society.

Hopefully, this chapter will help us recoup the uniqueness and importance of this sacramental encounter with the healing Jesus. It will arm us with reasons that will assist in our efforts at evangelization of others about the sacrament. Each follower of Jesus must personally make this sacramental encounter appealing for our generation and bring souls to God's tender mercy. In effect, confession must be or become an integral part of our lives as Catholics. If it is not, we are failing to live our faith and explore all its resources to the fullest. Catholic teaching is clear: "Individual and integral confession of grave sins followed by absolution remains the only ordinary means of reconciliation with God and with the Church" (CCC 1497).

The sacrament must, moreover, be readily available in our parishes. In addition, each of us should personally invite our fellow Catholics to experience this encounter of mercy. If they have been away, we pray that, once returned to this sacramental encounter, they will receive the sacrament on a regular basis. The example of each one of us, priest and lay, is of paramount importance. *Nemo dat quod non habet* (No one can give what one does not have).

A Very Personal Sacrament

In the first order, it is the will of Jesus that his healing continues in the life of the Church through his priests. It is Christ, in the person of the priest, who actually forgives sins and heals us. "The Lord Jesus Christ, physician of our souls and bodies . . . has willed that his Church continue, in the power of the Holy Spirit, his work of healing and salvation (CCC 1421)" (*USCCA* 234). This authority was given to the apostles on that first Easter Sunday night by the risen Lord: "Receive the holy Spirit. Whose sins you forgive are forgiven them, and whose sins you retain are retained" (Jn 20:22–23).

In the words of Archbishop Donald Wuerl:

> There is a comforting simplicity to confession. With sincere contrition we need only open our hearts to the priest, recount our failings and ask forgiveness. What follows is one of those moments in the life of the Church when the awesome power of Jesus Christ is most clearly and directly felt. In the name of the Church and Jesus Christ, the priest absolves the penitent from sin. At the heart of confession is the momentous action of absolution that only a priest can grant by invoking the authority of the Church and acting in the person of Jesus Christ.

This sacrament is a personal encounter with Jesus, the healing Jesus, the same Jesus (in the person of the priest) who spent a great part of his life on earth healing and forgiving. The sacrament of Penance is extremely personal. Sins cannot be faxed, e-mailed, or delivered by FedEx. A number of years ago, speaking to the French Bishops, our late Holy Father John Paul II said this about the sacrament of Penance:

> At a period in which private life is extolled and people wish to protect it against the pressures and the anonymity of large human groups, the act of confessing one's sins and receiving from God a word of forgiveness addressed personally to each individual is to proclaim that, in the human race, each one counts before God.

As you think about this sacrament, its very personal nature, the potential for genuine and deep healing, think of the life of the historical Jesus. Think, above all, of his miracles. This sacrament is the open door to miracles in our lives, too. This is a sacrament of miracles. It is the grace of conversion, that gradual and daily change of life that it offers.

When you pull back the velvet curtain or open the door to the reconciliation room, think of Jesus healing the paralytic at Capernaum. This man was lowered through the ceiling to the feet of Jesus because his friends—who overcame all obstacles to bring this man to Jesus—were unable to get to Jesus directly through the front door. Before Jesus healed him and told him, "Pick up your mat, and go home," he said to him, "My son, your sins are forgiven" (Mk 2:9–11). That shows the priority given to the forgiveness of sins, even over the physical healing of the paralysis. In effect, there was a deeper paralysis, the paralysis of sin. For Jesus, the priority was, and continues to be, the forgiveness of sin, the healing of the paralysis of sin that takes hold in each of us from time to time. This gospel passage also underscores that each of us, without exception, is challenged to be involved in the ministry of reconciliation. The paralyzed man could not have come to Jesus unaided. It was his friends, friends hopefully like you and me, that overcame the physical obstacles to bring him to Jesus. The crowd had never seen anything quite like this before.

Or consider the woman caught in the very act of adultery in John 8! Such beautiful, healing, and miraculous language is used by Jesus in the face of the scribes and Pharisees who wanted to stone her. "Neither do

I condemn you. Go and from now on do not sin any more."

Or think of the prodigal son from the Gospel of St. Luke, perhaps better titled "the merciful father." The *United States Catholic Catechism for Adults* describes it in these words: "Christ's parable of the prodigal son illustrates the sublime meaning of his earthly ministry, which is to forgive sins, reconcile people to God, and lead us to true happiness (cf. Lk 15:11–32)" (*USCCA* 235).

Even from the pulpit of the Cross, so central to our Lenten pilgrimage each year, comes the language of healing and forgiveness and mercy. Remember the penitent criminal hanging next to Jesus and Jesus' words: "Amen, I say to you, today you will be with me in Paradise" (Lk 23:43). Such consoling words of healing and forgiveness from the gibbet of the Cross as Jesus hung dying! Yes, Jesus, as it were, hearing confessions from the very Cross itself, the Cross from which our salvation was won. There was no dichotomy between the words of Jesus and his actions.

For many of us, the real issue is the word *sin*. It is not a politically correct word in our day. Many of us have lost the meaning of it. Before talking about the sacrament that continues the healing mission of Jesus, a mission that is central to the Church's task, perhaps a word should be said about what needs healing. "The Sacrament of Penance must be seen within the context of conversion from sin and a turn to God" (*USCCA* 236).

A Sense of Sin

Not much emphasis has been placed on the reality of sin, with its mystery, paralysis, and burden, in

Catholic preaching and teaching over the last twenty-five years. In sharp contrast, the Catechism gives much attention to sin.

Lent is the time of year, par excellence, to focus on the mystery of sin in our lives—that gnawing, debilitating, and paralyzing sin, that *one* sin perhaps that eats away at us and deprives us of a full life with God. That need not be. Lent is that special time to correct that sin, to recoup the sense of sin in our lives, and to experience ever anew his mercy with the assurance that our sins are actually forgiven no matter how often we confess the same sin or set of sins.

The Catechism teaches that "after that first sin, the world is virtually inundated by sin" (CCC 401). This should not surprise any of us. If we think about it, however, it is much easier to live in denial regarding the existence of sin. It is much easier to dismiss the constant din of sirens that sound throughout our urban areas every night, the sound of guns, the cry for help of an innocent person, the expanding drug culture, the high divorce rate, churches far short of capacity on Sunday. "After that first sin, the world is virtually inundated by sin."

Our Church teaches the reality of personal sin and original sin. It teaches that as a result of original sin, that first sin, human nature is weakened in its powers. We are more inclined to sin, subject to ignorance, suffering, and the domination of death. Original sin is not a sin "committed," but rather "contracted" (CCC 404). It is a state, not an act. And each one of us without exception is a recipient of this transmission from our first parents.

It is a deprivation of original holiness and justice. Wounded human nature results. Genesis says, after our first parents disobeyed and ate the fruit from the tree of the knowledge of good and evil, "then the eyes of both of them were opened, and they realized that they were naked; so they sewed fig leaves together and made loincloths for themselves" (Gen 3:7). They were full of shame and guilt.

There is still a tree of the knowledge of good and evil in each of our lives. God continues to tell us, "You shall not eat it or even touch it, lest you die." These are God's words to our first parents and to each of us. Death results when we disobey, when we sin.

That tree symbolically represents the insurmountable limits that we must freely recognize and respect with trust. Sin results when we trust ourselves at the expense of God. Sin results when we live as if God's Word did not exist. Sin results when we ignore the limits set for us in the Ten Commandments, the Beatitudes, and the moral teaching of the Church and resort to our own devices and the alleged "solutions" that the world proposes. Sin is a rejection of God who is the only true, living tree of life. Sin is a preference by and for man and his human devices instead of a preference for God.

"Sin is before all else an offense against God, a rupture of communion with him. At the same time, it damages communion with the Church" (CCC 1440).

Despite our weakened state and our proclivity to sin, as followers of Jesus, we live in hope. Pope Benedict XVI, in his encyclical on hope, cited St. Paul: "In hope we were saved" (SS 1). That is, after all, our Christian inheritance. Death does not have the last word. St. Paul says it so well: "For if, by the transgression of one person, death came to reign through that one, how much more will those who receive the abundance of grace and

of the gift of justification come to reign in life through
the one person Jesus Christ" (Rom 5:17).

A Call to Conversion

Jesus died that our sins might be forgiven—each and
every sin. And the sacrament of Penance is precisely
where as Catholics we share in the healing and forgiving fruits of his death out of love for us. It is a sacrament
of conversion, confession, and forgiveness.

The Catechism lists the various names used for this
sacrament over the years—each reflecting a different
emphasis given to that same sacrament. I believe that
the change in name for this sacrament has in part been
responsible for the misunderstanding of this sacrament.
The healing sacrament has been called:

> *The sacrament of conversion,* because it ritual-
> izes the "turning around" to the Father, rich
> in mercy, of one who has sinned.

> *The sacrament of Penance,* which places pri-
> mary focus on the satisfaction or the pen-
> ance one is given by the priest at the end of
> the celebration.

> *The sacrament of confession or simply "confes-
> sion,"* which underscores the actual disclo-
> sure or confession of sins to the priest, which
> is an essential part of the sacrament.

> *The sacrament of forgiveness,* since by the
> priest's sacramental absolution, the penitents

receive "pardon and peace," an assurance that our sins are in fact forgiven and that we are ready for a new lease on life.

The sacrament of Reconciliation, because it imparts to the sinner the love of God, who alone reconciles. The sacrament involves both a horizontal reconciliation with one's brothers and sisters *and* a vertical reconciliation with God. (*CCC* 1423–1424)

At the heart of each of these names and at the very basis of this sacrament, however, is the call to conversion. It is Jesus' repeated call to conversion. The very first words of his public ministry are in Mark 1:15, the words used on Ash Wednesday during the distribution of ashes: "The reign of God is at hand. Reform your lives and believe in the gospel." Throughout his whole public ministry, Jesus takes very seriously this call to repentance and reform. "This call is an essential part of the proclamation of the kingdom" (*CCC* 1427).

"Reform" comes from the Greek word *metanoia,* which means repentance, conversion, and change of heart. Repentance, indeed conversion, is a graced event. The first conversion is at Baptism. The second conversion is that daily ongoing process of turning to the Lord and away from sin, greatly aided by the regular reception of the sacrament of Reconciliation. The Catechism makes clear that it "is not just a human work. It is the movement of a 'contrite heart' drawn and moved by grace to respond to the merciful love of God who loved us first" (*CCC* 1428).

The Catechism states: "Interior repentance is a radical reorientation of our whole life, a return, a conversion to God with all our heart, an end of sin, a turning away from evil, with repugnance toward the evil actions we have committed. At the same time, it entails the desire and resolution to change one's life, with hope in God's mercy and trust in the help of his grace" (CCC 1431).

"The human heart is heavy and hardened. God must give man a new heart . . . God gives us the strength to begin anew" (CCC 1432). Repentance is ultimately the Lord's work in our lives, but it requires our own cooperation.

How often at our parish penance services do we sing "Grant to us, O Lord, a heart renewed," or how often do we pray Psalm 51?

> A pure heart create for me, O God,
> put a steadfast spirit within me.
> Do not cast me away from your presence,
> nor deprive me of your Holy Spirit. (12–13)

"Christ instituted the sacrament of Penance for all sinful members of his Church: above all for those who, since Baptism, have fallen into grave sin, and have thus lost their baptismal grace and wounded ecclesial communion. It is to them that the sacrament of Penance offers a new possibility to convert and recover the grace of justification. The Fathers of the Church present this sacrament as 'the second plank [of salvation] after the shipwreck which is the loss of grace'" (CCC 1446, brackets from CCC).

"The Sacrament of Penance is an experience of the gift of God's boundless mercy. Not only does it free us from our sins but it also challenges us to have the same kind of compassion and forgiveness for those who sin against us" (USCCA 242). We remember the words of the Our Father: "Forgive us our sins as we forgive those who sin against us." To the extent that we forgive others, our merciful Father will forgive us our sins.

The Rite of Penance

Although there have been changes in name, discipline, and the manner of celebration of this sacrament over the centuries (and even since the conclusion of Vatican II), the same fundamental structure exists. "It comprises two equally essential elements: on the one hand, the acts of the man who undergoes conversion through the action of the Holy Spirit: namely, contrition, confession, and satisfaction; on the other, God's action through the intervention of the Church" (CCC 1448).

There are four essential elements to this sacrament:

> *Contrition*, sorrow for one's sins with a determination to avoid sin in the future. This is not a matter of feelings. It is a matter of will.

> *Confession (disclosure) of one's sins.* With the admission of our sins, we take responsibility for them. The penitent opens himself / herself again to God and the Church in the person of the priest in order to make a new future possible. Before confessing one's sins, there is need for an examination of conscience that requires a certain ongoing formation of conscience. The number and types of sins should be stated. "All mortal sins of which penitents after a diligent self-examination are conscious must be recounted by them in confession" (CCC 1456). "Without being

strictly necessary, confession of everyday faults (venial sins) is nevertheless strongly recommended by the Church" (CCC 1458). The Catechism is also clear on the following point:

> "After having attained the age of discretion, each of the faithful is bound by an obligation faithfully to confess serious sins at least once a year" (CIC, can. 989). Anyone who is aware of having committed a mortal sin must not receive Holy Communion, even if he experiences deep contrition, without having first received sacramental absolution, unless he has a grave reason for receiving Communion and there is no possibility of going to confession. Children must go to the sacrament of Penance before receiving Holy Communion for the first time. (CCC 1457)

Absolution. When given by the priest, "sets us free from our sins, using the power that Christ entrusted to the Church and by which he pardons the sins of the penitent" (USCCA 240). With absolution, there is an assurance that our sins are forgiven.

Satisfaction (Penance), something the penitent is called to do by the confessor to atone for his or her sins. It is also referred to as penance. It is intended to assist in the healing and not be punitive. There is often a communitarian dimension, since so many of our sins affect others also, and harm must be repaired. "Just as when we get physically out of shape, we need to take up some exercise, so also when the soul is morally out of shape, there is the challenge to adopt spiritual exercises that will restore it" (USCCA 240).

I invite those of you who have not received the healing grace of the sacrament of Reconciliation in a long time to come, to open the door to this sacrament of Jesus' healing mercy. Come in and be not afraid! For those of you who receive the sacrament regularly, I encourage you to continue and to talk about it with others. Encourage them. Bring them with you to the sacrament. It is a wonderful spiritual work of mercy, a genuine act of charity to bring someone back to this sacrament, particularly a family member.

Each day at Morning Prayer, the Church prays the Canticle of Zechariah. I conclude this chapter with the memorable words of Zechariah, who prophesied to his son John the Baptist: "For you will go before the Lord to prepare his way, to give his people knowledge of salvation by the forgiveness of their sins" (Lk 1:77). Precisely in the forgiveness of our sins in sacramental confession do we come to a deeper awareness of our salvation. We come to know there and most uniquely and ever anew and with assurance that we have and are being saved from ourselves and our darker side. That *is* Good News.

Reflect

1. What was your childhood experience with the sacrament of Penance like? How does it affect you today?

2. What are some of the benefits you have experienced in going to confession?

3. In what ways have you found Penance to be a healing sacrament?

4. What does it mean for you to say these words at Mass: "Lord, I am not worthy to receive you, but only say the word and I shall be healed"?

Pray

Psalm 51

Have mercy on me, God, in your kindness.
In your compassion blot out my offense.
O wash me more and more from my guilt
and cleanse me from my sin.
My offenses truly I know them;
my sin is always before me.
Against you, you alone, have I sinned;
what is evil in your sight I have done.
That you may be justified when you give
    sentence
and be without reproach when you judge,
O see, in guilt I was born,
a sinner was I conceived.
Indeed you love truth in the heart;

then in the secret of my heart teach me
   wisdom.
O purify me, then I shall be clean;
O wash me, I shall be whiter than snow.
Make me hear rejoicing and gladness,
that the bones you have crushed may thrill.
From my sins turn away your face
and blot out all my guilt.
A pure heart create for me, O God,
put a steadfast spirit within me.
Do not cast me away from your presence,
nor deprive me of your holy spirit.
Give me again the joy of your help;
with a spirit of fervor sustain me,
that I may teach transgressors your ways
and sinners may return to you.
O rescue me, God, my helper,
and my tongue shall ring out your
   goodness.
O Lord, open my lips
and my mouth shall declare your praise.
For in sacrifice you take no delight,
burnt offering from me you would refuse,
my sacrifice, a contrite spirit,
a humbled, contrite heart you will not
   spurn.

SEVEN

Another Healing Sacrament: The Anointing of the Sick

Regrettably, there is no sacrament more poorly understood in our time than the beautiful healing sacrament of the Anointing of the Sick. It is intended to strengthen and confer a special grace on those being tried by illness, a population that Jesus was attracted to like a magnet in his public ministry. In this sacrament, Jesus' healing ministry, indeed his preferential ministry to the sick, continues in our day. Jesus has often been portrayed, after all, as the Divine Physician. Moreover, he also sent his disciples to heal the sick. Thus "Jesus did not only send his disciples forth to heal the sick (cf. Mt 10:8; Lk 9:2, 10:9); he also instituted a specific sacrament for them: the Anointing of the Sick. The Letter of James attests to the presence of this sacramental sign in the early Christian community (cf. 5:14–16)" (SC 22).

"This sacred anointing of the sick was instituted by Christ our Lord as a true and proper sacrament of the New Testament. It is alluded to indeed by Mark [6:13], but is recommended to the faithful and promulgated by James the apostle and brother of the Lord" (CCC 1511). In the letter of James, we hear the question and command: "Are any among you sick? Let them call for the presbyters of the Church, and let them pray over them, anointing them with oil in the name of the Lord; and the prayer of faith will save the sick, and the Lord will raise them up; and if they have committed sins, they will be forgiven" (Jas 5:14–15). This is the biblical foundation of the sacrament of the Anointing of the Sick.

Since coming to my large and thriving suburban parish that includes many seniors in addition to young families, I have been reintroduced as a priest to this beautiful sacrament in so many different circumstances—those preparing for serious surgery, individuals seriously ill, or those who are terminally ill. The requests have come during the day and in the middle of the night. Regardless of the hour, it is truly an opportunity for a priest to be present sacramentally at a most important time in a person's life.

It is a sacrament that hopefully will be rediscovered in our day. Importantly, it is up to each faithful Catholic to call the priest if a person is seriously ill or near death, suffering the difficulties of old age, or about to have serious surgery. It is truly a form of evangelization!

The Contemporary Understanding of the Sacrament

Formerly, this sacrament was popularly referred to as Extreme Unction, and it was practically considered a deathbed sacrament. A family member would typically call the priest when a loved one or family member was near death.

Understood today, the Anointing of the Sick can be administered at various moments.

> [It] is not a sacrament for those only who are at the point of death. Hence, as soon as any

> one of the faithful begins to be in danger of
> death from sickness or old age, the fitting
> time for him to receive this sacrament has
> certainly already arrived" (SC 73). . . . It is fit-
> ting to receive the Anointing of the Sick just
> prior to a serious operation. The same holds
> for the elderly whose frailty becomes more
> pronounced. (CCC 1514–15)

In addition, "if during the same illness the person's
condition becomes more serious, the sacrament may be
repeated" (CCC 1515).

In fact, in addition to prayers for those in extreme
illness or advanced age, the Rites of Anointing include
a specific prayer before surgery that includes prayer for
the surgeon. I used this prayer for a young person in
the parish just prior to the time of his surgery: "We pray
that through the skills of surgeons and nurses your healing gifts may be granted [to that person]." He happily
recovered well and is now about to begin high school.
This holy sacramental anointing can be given at home,
at the church, or in a hospital or nursing home.

Only a priest or bishop, however, may administer
this sacrament using the Oil of the Sick blessed by the
bishop at the Chrism Mass. The forehead and hands of
the sick person are anointed, and the celebrant recites
the prayer of anointing. The hoped-for effect is that the
person will be physically healed, if it is God's will. At its
heart, however, even if the desired healing does not take
effect, a more radical healing does: "the victory over sin
and death through his Passover" (CCC 1505). The Catechism speaks at length about the various effects of this
sacrament.

The Graces of the Sacrament

Each sacrament has specific graces. The first grace of the sacrament of Anointing of the Sick is the gift of the Holy Spirit. It is a grace that strengthens and gives peace and courage to assist a person in overcoming the condition of serious illness or the frailty of old age. "This grace is a gift of the Holy Spirit, who renews trust and faith in God and strengthens against the temptation to discouragement and anguish in the face of death" (CCC 1520). Furthermore, "if he has committed sins, he will be forgiven" if the person was unable to receive the sacrament of Penance (CCC 1520). For this latter effect, the necessity of the priest as celebrant of this sacrament is underscored.

There is also a second grace of uniting the sick person more closely to Christ's Passion, and thus "in a certain way he is consecrated to bear fruit by configuration to the Savior's redemptive Passion" (CCC 1521). A deeper understanding of suffering hopefully takes hold in the sick person. Through this sacrament, a person actually shares in the redemptive suffering of Christ. "Suffering, a consequence of original sin, acquires a new meaning; it becomes a participation in the saving work of Jesus" (CCC 1521). St. Paul teaches that the sufferings we endure can "complete what is lacking in Christ's afflictions for the sake of his body, that is, the Church" (Col 1:24).

There is another grace that comes from this sacrament called an "ecclesial grace"—a grace for the Church. "By celebrating this sacrament the Church, in the communion of saints, intercedes for the benefit of the sick person, and he, for his part, through the grace of this sacrament, contributes to the sanctification of the Church and to the good of all men for whom the Church suffers and offers herself through Christ to God the Father" (*CCC* 1522).

Finally, this sacrament, when celebrated for those departing this life, completes our conformity to the death and Resurrection of the Lord Jesus as Baptism began it. "This last anointing fortifies the end of our earthly life like a solid rampart for the final struggles before entering the Father's house" (*CCC* 1523). The Eucharist, called viaticum, can also be received at this time. The Eucharist is understood here as "the sacrament of the passing over from death to life, from this world to the Father" (*CCC* 1524). Pope Benedict reminds us:

> On their journey to the Father, communion in the Body and Blood of Christ appears as the seed of eternal life and the power of Resurrection: "Anyone who eats my flesh and drinks my blood has eternal life and I will raise him up on the last day" (Jn 6:54). Since viaticum gives the sick a glimpse of the fullness of the Paschal mystery, its administration should be readily provided for. Attentive pastoral care shown to those who are ill brings great spiritual benefit to the entire community, since whatever we do to one of the least of our brothers and sisters, we do to Jesus himself (cf. Mt 25:40). (*SC* 22)

In summary, "the gifts of this Sacrament include uniting the sick person with Christ's Passion, for the person's well-being and that of the Church; strength to endure patiently the sufferings of illness and old age;

the forgiveness of sins if the person was unable to receive the Sacrament of Penance; and preparation for the passage to eternal life" (USCCA 257–58). The Anointing of the Sick is a beautiful sacramental encounter with Christ. It takes place at a special time in one's life when such an encounter clearly enables one to be uniquely joined to him who out of love suffered and died for each one of us.

Reflect

1. If you have received the sacrament of the Anointing of the Sick, describe what the experience was like for you.

2. Would you feel any reluctance about asking for the sacrament of the Anointing of the Sick for yourself or a family member? Why or why not?

3. What are the different ways that one might experience the healing effect of the Anointing of the Sick?

4. A popular Catholic saying, "Offer it up," has largely fallen out of use today. Does the idea of offering one's suffering to God for the good of oneself or others have a place in your spiritual life?

Pray

A Living Sacrifice

Teach me, Lord God,
to offer my body as a living sacrifice to you:
my head, my arms, my legs;
my conscious and my unconscious—
impulses, thoughts, desires, ambitions—
all the known and unknown
that make up the real me.
Teach me, also,
to offer those parts of my body
which are sick and disabled.
Cleanse me, heal me,
and renew me by your Spirit.
Through the offering of your beloved Son
on the cross of Calvary,
may the offering of my body
be a spiritual act of worship
holy and pleasing to you.

—John Gunstone

EIGHT

Holy Orders: Apostolic Ministry

I would like to begin this chapter with a prayerful description of the priest from the nineteenth-century French Dominican Henri Lacordaire:

> To live in the midst of the world without wishing its pleasures; to be a member of each family, yet belonging to none; to share all sufferings; to penetrate all secrets; to heal all wounds; to go from people to God and offer him their prayers; to return from God to people to bring pardon and hope; to have a heart of fire for charity and a heart of bronze for chastity; to teach and to pardon, console and bless always, My God what a life! And it is yours, O Priest of Jesus Christ!

Both the *Catechism of the Catholic Church* and the *United States Catholic Catechism for Adults* refer to the sacraments of Holy Orders and Matrimony as the "Sacraments at the Service of Communion." And "this means they are primarily directed toward the salvation of others. The recipients of these sacraments grow in holiness through their service to others" (*USCCA* 262–63; *CCC* 1534). Indeed they both are service sacraments, sacraments directed toward the salvation of others: for married people—to one's spouse and family, and for those ordained—to the greater family of the Church.

Both of these sacraments complement each other. As a priest, I have observed how the faithful commitment of husbands and wives in marriage can be a wonderful strength to those of us in the priesthood as we seek faithfully to live out our call to celibacy. Married couples have told me that it works the other way as well. After all, we are each, in our respective vocations, called to building up the Church in different ways and giving glory to God.

"Holy Orders is the sacrament through which the mission entrusted by Christ to his apostles continues to be exercised in the Church until the end of time: thus it is the sacrament of apostolic ministry. It includes three degrees: episcopate [bishop], presbyterate [priest], and the diaconate [deacon]" (CCC 1536).

The Catechism makes it clear that these "ministries conferred by ordination are irreplaceable for the organic structure of the Church: without the bishop, presbyters, and deacons, one cannot speak of the Church" (CCC 1593).

Bishops and Priests

A bishop receives *"the fullness of the sacrament of Holy Orders"* (CCC 1557) and becomes a successor of the apostles. That means he can ordain men to the priesthood and consecrate men as bishops. A priest cannot do this. By his consecration, he is integrated into the entire episcopal college, as a successor of the apostles. Indeed, bishops are "transmitters of the apostolic line" (CCC 1555). Each one has responsibility not only for his own geographical diocese or office but for the whole Church. As an authentic teacher of the faith, the bishop strives to "guard the rich trust with the help of the Holy Spirit that dwells among us" (2 Tm 1:14).

By ordination, every priest is a co-worker of the bishop. Priests share, to a "subordinate degree," in the ministry of the bishop (CCC 1562). In a certain sense, the priest—who together with his bishop and the priests of the individual diocese form a unique priestly college—represents the bishop. A priest can exercise his ministry only in dependence on the bishop and in communion with him to whom he has taken a promise of respect and obedience. "Through that sacrament [Holy Orders] priests by the anointing of the Holy Spirit are signed with a special character and so are configured to Christ the priest in such a way that they are able to act in the person of Christ the head" (CCC 1563).

There is a wonderful fraternity among priests. I have experienced this and am daily sustained by priest friends around the world. It is aptly described in this anonymous reflection titled "The Brotherhood of Priests":

> There happens to be in this world of strange social conventions one friendship that transcends all conventions and knows no rules. It is the brotherhood of Catholic priests. There is not, I swear it, under the stars an intimacy more reckless or more profound than the bond between one priest and another.
>
> It needs no coaxing, no prelude, no ritual. It is subject to no formality. We meet and possess one another instantly. There is no shadow of a barrier between us, neither age,

nor antecedents, nor nationality, nor climate,
nor color of skin. Ours is a blunt, rough-
hewn affection.

His home is my home; his fireside, my
fireside; his altar, my altar. I can give him
my confidences promptly and without re-
serve. I can neither edify nor scandalize him.
We can quarrel without offense, praise each
other without flattery—sit silently and say
nothing.

How and why all this can happen is our
own secret. It is the secret of men who climb
a lonely drawbridge, mount a narrow stair,
sleep in a lofty citadel that floats a white flag.
Singly we go, independent and unpossessed,
establishing no generation, each a conclusion to his race and name, yet always com-
panioning each other with strange sympathy,
too tender to be called fellowship, too stur-
dy to be called love, but for which God will
find a name when he searches our hearts in
eternity.

The sacrament of Holy Orders was prefigured in the
Old Testament. Melchizedek was the first priest figure
in the Hebrew scriptures. He offered a sacrifice of bread
and wine on behalf of the patriarch Abraham and is
a symbol of the permanence of the priesthood. "Like
Melchizedek you are a priest forever" (Ps 110:4). Aaron
and his sons were chosen to be priests. From the twelve
tribes, one tribe, that of the Levites, was designated the
priestly tribe of Israel. They were to serve the people
in a special way liturgically and as leaders of prayer.
"The priesthood of Melchizedek, Aaron, and the Levites

prefigured the priesthood of Christ, as is seen in consecration prayers for the ordination of bishops, priests and deacons" (*USCCA* 264).

Christ, Our High Priest

Everything that the priesthood of the Old Testament prefigured is fulfilled in Christ Jesus, who alone is the one mediator between God and man. The Old Testament priests were unable to provide the fullness of salvation or the definitive sanctification for the people. Only Jesus Christ could do this. He is, after all, the High Priest who continually intercedes for us at the right hand of the Father precisely as a result of the Easter victory.

In Preface III for the Easter Season we pray: "He is still our priest, our advocate who always pleads our cause. Christ is the victim who dies no more, the Lamb, once slain, who lives forever."

It is important to realize that Christ has made each of us—each and every baptized Christian—a sharer in his priesthood. "The whole Church is [thus] a priestly people. Through Baptism all the faithful share in the priesthood of Christ. This participation is called the 'common priesthood of the faithful.' Based on this common priesthood and ordered to its service, there exists another participation in the mission of Christ: the ministry conferred by the sacrament of Holy Orders" (*CCC* 1591).

This is called the ministerial priesthood. It differs in essence and degree from the common priesthood of all the baptized because it confers a special sacred power by ordination. Christ calls all the baptized—those who share in the common priesthood—to share in the

Spirit's work of "sanctifying the world." Christ calls the
ordained or ministerial priesthood uniquely to share
in the Spirit's work of "sanctifying the faithful." In the
words of St. John Vianney: "The priesthood is the love
of the heart of Jesus" (CCC 1589).

"The ordained or *ministerial* priesthood is at the service of the baptismal priesthood. The ordained priesthood guarantees that it really is Christ who acts in the
sacraments through the Holy Spirit for the Church"
(CCC 1120). Essential to the ministerial priesthood is
the conferral of the unique power of consecrating and
offering the true Body and Blood of Christ at Mass, of
forgiving sins after Baptism through the sacraments of
Penance and the Anointing of the Sick. In this sacramental ministry, it is "Christ himself who is present to
his Church as Head of his Body, Shepherd of his flock,
high priest" (CCC 1548).

The priesthood is a gift of God for his Church. It
is a "call," a call that comes from God alone. It is a
great mystery. "The ministerial priesthood is a means
by which Christ unceasingly builds up and leads his
Church" (CCC 1547). A priest acts *in persona Christi*, in
the very person of Christ.

> An image used to explain this reality talks
> of a priest as an "icon" of Christ. An icon
> is a religious painting that is considered to
> make present the mystery of salvation or the
> saint it depicts. To say a priest is an icon of
> Christ means, then, that a priest is not just a
> reminder or image of Christ but is also a real
> means by which a person can be touched by
> Christ. Because Christ is a man, it is fitting

that a priest as the icon of Christ should also be a man. (*USCCA* 268)

This ministerial priesthood is a unique and special share in our day, in every age, in the mission of Jesus himself, Jesus the Good Shepherd. Jesus was not only priest, he was also prophet and king. And the ordained priest shares in that very same mission in a special and unique way.

His share in the mission of Jesus is not simply a theological construct. Jesus' mission now becomes each priest's mission in concrete and real terms each and every day. But how?

The Mission of Jesus as Priest

Jesus the high priest stands victoriously now at the right hand of the Father interceding for each and every one of us—the one and only mediator between God and man. A priest stands *in persona Christi* (in the person of Christ). He is most a priest (and he shares in Christ's own priesthood) at the altar of sacrifice, at Holy Mass—the root of every priest's life. Referring to priests, the Catechism states that at the Eucharist "they exercise in a supreme degree their sacred office" (CCC 1566). It is at the altar where the relation of priesthood to Christ's ultimate act of love for us on the Cross is spelled out dramatically. There, the consecration of the bread and wine into the Body and Blood of Christ "re-presents" (in an unbloody way) the sacrifice of Calvary offered once and for all by Christ for our salvation—the lasting memorial of his presence among us. That is what takes place at every Mass.

At Mass, the priest calls upon the Holy Spirit that the gifts of bread and wine might become the Body and Blood of our Lord Jesus Christ (and this is the unique privilege and obligation of the priest). He likewise prays that we might share in Jesus' dying and rising every time we eat this bread, the bread of life, and drink this cup, the cup of eternal salvation. The Eucharist is nourishment for our daily journey of faith and the "source and summit" of our lives as Christians.

The late and beloved John Cardinal O'Connor of New York wrote beautifully about this:

> It's in the offering of the sacrifice of the Mass, of course, that the priest reaches his fullness, the bishop reaches his fullness. What could one possibly do that would be comparable to taking the place of Christ in the Mass, saying over a piece of bread, "this is my body," over a cup of wine, "this is my blood." That's really when we all come into our fullness.

In his letter proclaiming the Year for Priests (June 16, 2009), Benedict XVI quoted St. John Vianney:

> [He] spoke of the priesthood as if incapable of fathoming the grandeur of the *gift* and *task* entrusted to a human creature: "O, how great is the priest! . . . If he realized what he is, he would die. . . . God obeys him: he utters a few words and the Lord descends from heaven at his voice, to be contained within a small host."

The Mission of Jesus as Prophet

Like Jesus, the priest is a prophet in a long line of prophets from Isaiah to Jeremiah to Ezekiel. He is a prophet not in the commonly understood sense of a forecaster, someone who predicts future crises and catastrophes, but as one who falls in love with the Word of God found in Sacred Scripture and our living Catholic Tradition. A prophet preaches God's life-giving Word in season and out of season. He teaches. Importantly, he lives what he preaches. Therein lies his credibility. In his own prophetic way, Pope Paul VI wrote: "Modern man listens more willingly to witnesses than to teachers, and if he does listen to teachers, it is because they are witnesses" (*EN* 41).

It is the priest's task, as it was from the time of St. Peter, to "let the whole house of Israel know beyond any doubt that God has made both Lord and Messiah this Jesus whom you crucified" (Acts 2:36)—to be Easter witnesses to the world. Perhaps this is the most challenging part of Jesus' mission, the mission that the priest shares in our contemporary world. It is a world adopting more and more a culture of death instead of a culture of life, a world where secularism and materialism so often prevail, a world deaf to the gospel in so many places and ways. And yet it is uniquely a part of the work of priests to give prophetic witness from the pulpit and from their lives of the Good News that only Jesus can give.

The Mission of Jesus as King

Jesus was not a king as the world understands the term. Christ the King is best understood as the lamb on the throne slain for us. The blood of the lamb was shed for us that our sins might be forgiven. He is the victorious lamb whose precious blood makes true healing and reconciliation possible. The priest uniquely shares in Christ's kingly mission when he reconciles people in the sacrament of Penance, reconciling them to God, to neighbor, to the Church, and to themselves. And how important that is, in our increasingly broken world, a world that seems to feast on division, strife, and war!

Beyond the important work of sacramental reconciliation, a priest is a man of peace, one whose ministry it is to heal, reconcile, and unify a people, a parish, a community in the name of Jesus, to guide with a gentle arm and a shepherd's heart all those to whom he is sent—especially to the ill, the poor, and the most vulnerable.

Jesus *is* the exemplar, the ideal, the noble Shepherd after whom each priest is called to model his own life. He is the shepherd who "lays down his life for the sheep"—not just any sheep but those specifically sent for his care. He knows them and they know him. That is the life of a priest—to know well those to whom the Lord sends him to serve.

Five times in John's gospel, Jesus tells us that the Good Shepherd lays down his life for his sheep—so deep is his love. Unlike a hireling who has no concern for his sheep, Jesus, the Good Shepherd, proves his love. He gives his life that they might have life and life eternal.

In a special way, every priest is called to give over his life in celibate love for those he is called to serve. Like the Good Shepherd, he hears the pain of his people and knows when they need encouragement and love. Each priest is called to bring the weak close to his heart. He is the one who, after the example of the Good Shepherd, must from time to time leave the ninety-nine and go after the one who has strayed from the faith, from the Church. He is the one who knows and calls his people by name.

That is a priest's unique share in the kingly mission of Jesus.

This sharing in the triple mission of Jesus as priest, prophet, and king defines so well the role and identity of a priest in our day. Benedict XVI, in a general audience on July 1, 2009, at the beginning of the Year for Priests, spoke directly in another but related way to the identity and ministry of priests: "The two essential elements of priestly ministry" always remain "proclamation and power," said the Holy Father, recalling how Christ sent his disciples out to announce the gospel, giving them the power to drive out demons. "'Proclamation' and 'power,' that is, 'word' and 'sacrament,' are therefore the two basic pillars of priestly service, over and above its possible multiple circumstances."

A Call and a Gift

Once ordained a priest, a priest is a priest forever. Often we hear of priests who have left the active ministry or who have been laicized. But just as a baptized person cannot give up the indelible spiritual mark on his or her soul, which lasts forever, so, too, with the ordained priest. Even though he may no longer function as a priest, or for a very grave reason be forbidden to function as a priest, or be laicized and thus relieved of the responsibilities of a priest and even marry, he is still a priest forever.

A man responds to a call to priesthood. "When God chooses men to share in the ordained priesthood of Christ, he moves and helps them by his grace" (*USCCA* 269). It is thus both a call and a gift. In addition, all candidates for ordination in the Latin Church make a promise of celibacy "for the sake of the kingdom of heaven" (Mt 19:12). "Their celibacy is a sign of the intention to imitate Christ's own celibacy and to serve God in the Church's ministry with an undivided heart" (*USCCA* 270). There are two exceptions in the Latin Church: permanent deacons who are already married at the time of ordination, and in some cases married clergy of other Christian churches who convert to Catholicism and are admitted to Holy Orders.

The teaching that the ordained priesthood is reserved to men, after the example of Jesus, has been preserved by the constant and universal teaching of the Church. John Paul II affirmed this teaching in the following words: "In order that all doubt may be removed, I declare that the Church has no authority whatsoever to confer priestly ordination on women and that this judgment is to be definitively held by all the Church's faithful (*On Reserving Priestly Ordination to Men Alone* [*Ordinatio Sacerdotalis*], no. 4)" (*USCCA* 269).

The Diaconate

Having spoken of the episcopacy and the priesthood, we now turn to the first step in Holy Orders, which is that of deacon. It is also conferred by ordination by the bishop. Although deacons receive the sacrament of Holy Orders, they do not share in the ministerial priesthood but in a ministry of service. The word *deacon* comes from the Greek word *diakonia*, which means *service*. For a long time in the western Church, the diaconate was merely a next-to-last step toward priestly ordination. Like all priests, I was ordained to the transitional diaconate. Since Vatican II, however, the Latin-rite diaconate has been restored as a permanent order. It is the one order in the West that admits married men. Deacons—permanent and transitional—are ordained for a ministry of service. Deacons are ordained "not unto the priesthood, but unto the ministry" (CCC 1569). They have many roles: to celebrate the sacrament of Baptism; to witness marriages in the name of the Church; to preside at funeral and burial rites; to impart Benediction; to teach and preach the homily; and to do charitable and administrative work in connection with the Church.

I can personally attest that the restoration of the permanent diaconate has truly been an enrichment and blessing to the life of the Church, especially at the parish level. In both of the parishes where I have been privileged to serve as pastor, the permanent deacons have been of immeasurable assistance in service to the pastor and people. I am always happy to encourage other men to pray about and discern whether the Lord Jesus might be calling them to this ordained ministry of service.

In all three degrees, the episcopacy, priesthood, and diaconate, the sacrament of Holy Orders is conferred by the imposition of the bishop's hands and "a specific consecratory prayer asking God for the outpouring of the Holy Spirit and his gifts proper to the ministry to which the candidate is being ordained" (CCC 1573). An indelible spiritual character is imparted by this sacrament, a sacrament that cannot be repeated, not unlike Baptism and Confirmation.

A Priestly Heart

The Catechism makes it quite clear that no one has the right to receive the sacrament of Holy Orders—deacon, priest, or bishop. The call must come from God. It is a gift, above all. The Church has the responsibility and the authority, however, to do its best to verify that this call is from God and only then to call the person to receive Holy Orders.

I can firmly attest to the wonderful privilege it is "to be a member of each family, yet belonging to none" in the words of Father Lacordaire, and to be of service to God's holy Church, to be an instrument of his generous graces as a priest. Each of us is called daily to pray for our priests and pray ceaselessly for an increase in vocations.

The late Cardinal John O'Connor, a priest I very much admired, wrote in his own wonderful style:

> It's a wonderful time to be a priest. Some people don't trust us. Some think we're in it for the money. Some think celibacy is a lost art. Some think we're a dying breed.

So there's no question about the challenge. And who wants to go through life without a challenge? There's no such thing as a free lunch. We have to prove our honesty, our integrity, our decency, our loyalty every step of the way, and every day all over again. One of us slips and falls and makes headlines, and we're all on trial. That may make life a bit tough, at times, but it's really high praise. It suggests that after nearly two thousand years, people still expect us to be like Christ.

In a particular way, each and every priest, precisely because of his configuration to Christ by sacred ordination, is called to love Christ with his priestly heart. Reflecting this desire in his spiritual testament, my dear friend Cardinal Pio Laghi wrote just before his death on January 11, 2009: "I have wanted to love Christ and to serve him all my life, despite the fact that frequently my human fragility has impeded me from manifesting to him in an always recognizable way, as I would have wished, my love, my fidelity and my total surrender to his will." To seek to love Christ with all our hearts is the task of every baptized person and most especially those with a priestly heart.

Reflect

1. Is there a priest who has had a considerable impact on your life? In what way?

2. What words of encouragement would you give to a newly ordained priest?

3. How would you feel about a deacon performing a baptism, wedding, or wake service for a member of your family?

4. What would you say if your son, nephew, or grandchild told you he was thinking about entering the seminary?

Pray

Prayer for Vocations

Jesus, Son of God,
in whom the fullness of the Divinity dwells,
You call all the baptized to "put out into the
    deep,"
taking the path that leads to holiness.
Waken in the hearts of young people the
    desire
to be witnesses in the world of today
to the power of your love.
Fill them with your Spirit of fortitude and
    prudence,
so that they may be able to discover the full
    truth
about themselves and their own vocation.
Our Savior,
sent by the Father to reveal His merciful love,
give to your Church the gift
of young people who are ready to put out into
    the deep,
to be the sign among their brothers
of your presence which renews and saves.

Holy Virgin, Mother of the Redeemer,
sure guide on the way toward God and
    toward neighbor,
You who pondered his word in the depth of
    your heart,
sustain with your motherly intercession
our families and our ecclesial communities,
so that they may help adolescents and young
    people
to answer generously the call of the Lord.
    Amen.

—Pope John Paul II

NINE

Matrimony: It Takes Three

"I, John, take you Mary, to be my wife. I promise to be true to you in good times and in bad, in sickness and in health. I will love you and honor you all the days of my life." Then Mary says the same thing to John. Marriage takes place at that moment. The priest or deacon witnesses the vows and declares that what God has joined, we must not divide.

These or similar words have been uttered for many, many years in churches around the entire world. Many couples have repeated them, renewing their vows on a special anniversary. These words define and nurture a life-giving and lifelong relationship "in good times and bad, in sickness and in health."

What a wonderful joy it is to be the Church's witness as a priest or deacon at a marriage ceremony! It is likewise a genuine privilege and a real joy to help prepare a couple for their new vocation. Marriage, after all, is a unique vocation and sacrament. It is a special call from God. The couple leaves the marriage ceremony no longer two but "one flesh" in the Lord Jesus.

When two baptized persons, a man and a woman, marry each other, the Lord Jesus becomes an intimate partner of that union, that communion of man and woman. After all, in a marriage, as the title of this chapter states—"it takes three." In effect, the man and woman become married into Christ Jesus, for he has raised this covenant of two baptized persons to the dignity of a sacrament—one of seven unique and transformative encounters with our living God.

That is precisely what makes the marriage of two baptized persons, a Christian marriage, different from any other form of marriage. "The grace of the sacrament perfects the love of husband and wife, binds them together in fidelity, and helps them welcome and care for children. Christ is the source of this grace and he dwells with the spouses to strengthen their covenant promises, to bear each other's burdens with forgiveness and kindness, and to experience ahead of time the 'wedding feast of the lamb' (Rev 19:9)" (*USCCA* 285).

What then do these marriage vows mean? What does the Church understand about marriage? Marriage and family life are certainly under attack in our world today. One need only read the paper to see that efforts are being made to redefine the traditional understanding of marriage and sexuality. In fact, in his historic visit to Washington, D.C., Pope Benedict XVI spoke to the bishops of the United States and challenged America in these words, even after affirming the importance of family life: "How can we not be dismayed as we observe the sharp decline of the family as a basic element of Church and society? Divorce and infidelity have increased, and many young men and women are choosing to postpone marriage or to forego it altogether." He added, "To some young Catholics, the sacramental bond of marriage seems scarcely distinguishable from a civil bond, or even a purely informal and open-ended arrangement to live with another person."

That is why the *United States Catholic Catechism for Adults* states clearly:

> The Church and her members need to continue to be a strong and clear voice in protecting an understanding of marriage, which is rooted in natural law and revealed in God's law.... While the Church clearly teaches that discrimination against any group of people is wrong, efforts to make cohabitation, domestic partnerships, same-sex unions, and polygamous unions equal to marriage are misguided and also wrong. (*USCCA* 280)

This chapter will look systematically and fundamentally at the root meaning of marriage. It does this by focusing on holy Scripture and Tradition, which together set forth the meaning of marriage as the Church understands and teaches about marriage. Stated simply, it is a permanent union between a man and a woman. It is a loving union designed to give new life and life in the full.

God's Plan for Marriage

Both the *Catechism of the Catholic Church* and the *United States Catholic Catechism for Adults* can help us be better informed in our tackling and dealing with the challenging questions that marriage presents today and in every age. Such knowledge must always replace prejudice or ignorance.

The Catechism teaches:

> The vocation to marriage is written in the very nature of man and woman as they came

> from the hand of the Creator. Marriage is not a purely human institution despite the many variations it may have undergone through the centuries in different cultures, social structures, and spiritual attitudes. These differences should not cause us to forget its common and permanent characteristics. Although the dignity of this institution is not transparent everywhere with the same clarity, some sense of the greatness of matrimonial union exists in all cultures. (CCC 1603)

It is an integral part of our DNA.

The Catechism beautifully sets forth the Church's understanding of the intrinsic nature of marriage, sexuality, and family life. Importantly, it speaks of "God's plan" for marriage. For indeed God has a plan for marriage, and his plan stems from the very beginning of time. It is etched in the very order of creation itself. Genesis describes this so well. God is, after all, the author of marriage, and he has endowed marriage with its own laws.

In Genesis we read, "The Lord God said: 'It is not good for man to be alone. I will make a suitable partner for him'" (Gn 2:18). And the man said: "This one, at last, is bone of my bones and flesh of my flesh; this one shall be called 'woman.' . . . That is why a man leaves his father and mother and clings to his wife, and the two of them become one body" (Gn 2:23–24). God blessed the love between man and woman and said: "Be fertile and multiply" (Gn 1:28). From Genesis, the very first book of the Bible, to Revelation, the last book of the Bible, the language of marriage abounds. It is found in the creation narratives where God creates man and woman in his own image and likeness, and in the vision in Revelation of "the wedding feast of the lamb" (Rev 19:7).

Furthermore, Genesis describes a "rupture" in the love between a man and woman, a rupture that has come to be called Original Sin (CCC 1607). It was a rupture because God had intended and created man to live in loving communion with woman.

Marriage, then, from the very beginning, lives under the shadow of sin. This certainly reflects the reality of the human experience. The Catechism teaches:

> Every man experiences evil around him and within himself. This experience makes itself felt in the relationships between man and woman. This union has always been threatened by discord, a spirit of domination, infidelity, jealousy, and conflicts that can escalate into hatred and separation. (CCC 1606)

> The disorder . . . does not stem from the *nature* of man and woman, nor from the nature of their relations, but from *sin*. As a break with God, the first sin had for its first consequence the rupture of the original communion between man and woman. Their relations were distorted by mutual recriminations; their mutual attraction, the Creator's own gift, changed into a relationship of domination and lust; and the beautiful vocation of man and woman to be fruitful, multiply, and subdue the earth was burdened by the pain of childbirth and the toil of work. (CCC 1607)

From the beginning, Original Sin had direct and deleterious consequences for the love between a man and woman. Those consequences continue to this very day. Personal sin, especially when not repented, adversely affects the very purposes of marriage. Couples gradually find it easier to divorce or to be unfaithful rather than nurturing a faithful and exclusive relationship.

But there is Good News. It has a face, and that face is Jesus Christ's. By his life, death, Resurrection, and sending of the Spirit, Jesus undid the sin of Adam. And this will forever have a positive effect on each and every person baptized into him, inclusive of those who are called to the married state. This victory continues in our day in that special encounter with Jesus that is called sacramental confession. I cannot emphasize enough the special importance to married life of the regular reception of the sacrament of Penance. That frequent encounter with the healing Jesus is, after all, the fruit of the Easter mystery and a sure guarantee that married life will continue to deepen in surprising and miraculous ways. Forgiveness, another name for that sacrament, is the open door to miracles and an essential, miraculous ingredient in the deepening love between a man and woman joined together in marriage.

The Church's Teaching on Marriage

Throughout his ministry, Jesus always teaches by deeds and words. His words about marriage significantly complement the importance of his deeds, most specifically his presence at Cana.

> On the threshold of his public life Jesus
> performs his first sign—at his mother's re-
> quest—during a wedding feast (Jn 2:1–11).
> The Church attaches great importance to Je-
> sus' presence at the wedding at Cana. She
> sees in it the confirmation of the goodness of
> marriage and the proclamation that thence-
> forth marriage will be the efficacious sign of
> Christ's presence. (CCC 1613)

Clearly, there are Eucharistic overtones in this first
miracle of Jesus where he changed water into wine, in
much the same way as there are in the multiplication of
the loaves. Benedict XVI teaches, moreover, that there is
a relationship between the Eucharist and the sacrament
of Marriage. He writes that "the Eucharist inexhaust-
ibly strengthens the indissoluble unity and love of every Christian marriage. By the power of the sacrament,
the marriage bond is intrinsically linked to the Eucharistic unity of Christ the Bridegroom and his Bride, the
Church (cf. Eph 5:31–32)" (SC 27). How wonderful it
is to see so many couples, particularly as they grow
older together, at daily Mass! The Eucharist strengthens
their marital bonds and aids them in their growth in
holiness.

In his preaching, Jesus taught unequivocally about
the original meaning of the marriage covenant and
God's will that the covenant be indissoluble. When
asked about divorce, Jesus was explicitly clear that from
the very beginning of times—in fact quoting from Genesis and making it his own—he said, "'for this reason a
man shall leave his father and mother and be joined to
his wife, and the two shall become one flesh. So they are
no longer two, but one flesh.' Therefore, what God has

joined together, no human being must separate" (Mt. 19:4–7). This teaching of Jesus is an "unequivocal insistence on the indissolubility of the marriage bond" (*CCC* 1615). For Jesus, marriage is thus indissoluble, that is, forever, and there is a unity about it, that is, one flesh, a communion of persons.

At the same time, "Jesus has not placed on spouses a burden impossible to bear, or too heavy. . . . By coming to restore the original order of creation disturbed by sin, he himself gives the strength and the grace to live marriage in the new dimension of the Reign of God" (*CCC* 1615).

How is this possible?

> It is by following Christ, renouncing themselves, and taking up their crosses that spouses will be able to "receive" the original meaning of marriage and live it with the help of Christ. This grace of Christian marriage is a fruit of Christ's Cross, the source of all Christian life. (*CCC* 1615)

As I so often say in my marriage homilies, when one commits oneself to the other as husband or wife, Jesus also acts. He makes it possible. He gives the couple the capacity to love each other as he loved and continues to love his bride, the Church. The present love of the couple for each other will be strengthened by this sacramental encounter with Jesus. In fact, the new couple will be empowered anew to live the gospel commandment to love one another as the Lord Jesus loves us.

Marital love represents, in its deepest sense, the unbreakable love that Jesus had and continues to have for his Church, that new covenant of sacrificial love that

Jesus evidenced on the Cross, for his bride the Church, for each one of us.

That is the new law of love, the law of Christian marriage that forms the couples. St. Paul refers to this marital union as "a great mystery." He says, "I refer to Christ and his Church" (Eph 5:32). The sacrament of Marriage is akin to the loving, unbreakable, and totally self-giving love that Christ had and continues to have for his Church. The entire Christian life bears the mark of that spousal love of Christ and his Church.

That is why it is so appropriate, and normal between two Roman Catholics, to celebrate the sacrament of Marriage in the context of the Mass. "In the Eucharist the memorial of the New Covenant is realized, the New Covenant in which Christ has united himself forever to the Church, his beloved bride for whom he gave himself up. It is therefore fitting that the spouses should . . . give themselves to each other through the offering of their own lives by uniting it to the offering of Christ for his Church made present in the Eucharistic sacrifice" (CCC 1621).

The man and woman are the ministers of grace to one another. They confer the sacrament on each other by expressing their consent before the Christian community and in the presence of a deacon or priest who visibly represents the fact that marriage is an ecclesial reality. Gerald O'Collins and Mario Farrugia remind us: "Here matrimony stands apart from the other six sacraments, inasmuch as those who 'minister' the sacrament to each other are the bride and bridegroom." Integral to a valid Christian marriage is the consent. The Church teaches that "the exchange of consent between the spouses" is "the indispensable element that 'makes the marriage'" (CCC 1626).

The Two Purposes of Marriage

In addition, the marital union has a twofold end. They are "the good of the spouses themselves and the transmission of life" (CCC 2363).

With respect to the "good of the spouses," that means conjugal love itself. It is a love that is significantly different and more powerful than what the world typically understands by love, including sexual attraction, friendship, affection, relationship, and intimacy. It is all of those, but so much more. "By its very nature conjugal love requires the inviolable fidelity of the spouses. This is the consequence of the gift of themselves that they make to each other. Love seeks to be definitive; it cannot be an arrangement 'until further notice.' The 'intimate union of marriage, as a mutual giving of two persons, and the good of children demand total fidelity from the spouses and require an unbreakable union between them'" (CCC 1646). Our late Holy Father, John Paul II, in his apostolic letter *On the Dignity and Vocation of Women* wrote these very beautiful words: "In the 'unity of the two,' man and woman are called from the beginning not only to exist 'side by side' or 'together,' but they are also called *to exist mutually 'one for the other'*" (MD 7). What a profound way to describe married love! It is for the good of the spouses.

With respect to the second purpose of marriage, the transmission of life, what does this include? "By its very nature the institution of marriage and married love is ordered to the procreation and education of the offspring, and it is in them that it finds its crowning glory" (*CCC* 1652). Fecundity is a gift. It is a gift of God.

> So the Church, which "is on the side of life," teaches that "it is necessary that each and every marriage act must remain ordered *per se* to the procreation of human life. . . . This particular doctrine, expounded on numerous occasions by the Magisterium, is based on the inseparable connection, established by God, which man on his own initiative may not break, between the unitive significance and procreative significance which are both inherent to the marriage act." (*CCC* 2366)

In his 2009 encyclical letter *Charity in Truth* (*Caritas in Veritate*), Pope Benedict XVI reaffirmed this teaching, expressed clearly in Pope Paul VI's encyclical letter *Humanae Vitae* issued in 1968. But he also showed its connection to the Church's social teaching:

> The Encyclical *Humanae Vitae* emphasizes both the unitive and the procreative meaning of sexuality, thereby locating at the foundation of society the married couple, man and woman, who accept one another mutually, in distinction and in complementarity: a couple, therefore, that is open to life. This is not a question of purely individual morality: *Humanae Vitae* indicates the strong links between life ethics and social ethics, ushering in a new area of magisterial teaching that has gradually been articulated in a series of documents, most recently John Paul II's Encyclical *Evangelium Vitae*. The Church forcefully

maintains this link between life ethics and social ethics, fully aware that "a society lacks solid foundations when, on the one hand, it asserts values such as the dignity of the person, justice and peace, but then, on the other hand, radically acts to the contrary by allowing or tolerating a variety of ways in which human life is devalued and violated, especially where it is weak or marginalized (*EV* 101)." (*CV* 15)

Although the Church teaches responsible parenthood in the regulation of births, that does not mean, as some might suggest, an openness to life in marriage as a whole rather than such an openness in "each and every marital act" (*HV* 11). In God's mysterious plan, he calls married couples to live out their holiness in this latter way, that is, that each and every act of sexual intercourse must be open to new life. We keep coming back to the image of Christ's love for his Church—the model of married love. His Church, born on Calvary out of love, was a fruitful love. This is the model for the married state. The source of fruitfulness lies in the fact that no limit was placed on Christ's love for the Church. It was a total and full self-surrender. Married couples, like Jesus, witness to their call to holiness and grow in holiness when their love, without any artificial restriction, is total, fully human, exclusive, always open to new life and mutually self-giving. This union is more than physical fruitfulness. It means spiritual fruitfulness. It is that total surrender, one to the other, each and every day in both large and small matters. This is at the heart of married spirituality as the Church understands it.

Related Issues

In the midst of the discussion on marriage, both catechisms speak of "marriage preparation." They underscore the vital importance of marriage preparation. They link the very free and responsible consent, that indispensable aspect of marriage, to marriage preparation itself. "So that the 'I do' of the spouses may be a free and responsible act and so that the marriage covenant may have solid and lasting human and Christian foundations, preparation for marriage is of prime importance" (CCC 1632). "These programs are all the more necessary because cultural changes in recent times have undermined God's will for marriage" (USCCA 285).

As a priest, happily working with couples in their preparation for marriage, it has always been one of the most important parts of my ministry. These sessions with engaged couples are absolutely essential, and they can make a major difference for a couple in understanding exactly what it is that they are embarking upon, and hopefully, in the process, they come to know each other better.

Both catechisms also acknowledge a reality that is so clear from pastoral practice today—the presence of mixed marriages, that is, marriages between a Catholic and non-Catholic. Many couples, having received the appropriate permission, are living this kind of marital union and have done so very successfully for many years.

> Difference of confession between spouses does not constitute an insurmountable obstacle for marriage . . . but the difficulties of mixed marriages must not be underestimated. They arise from the fact that the

> separation of Christians has not yet been overcome . . . disparity of cult [marriage between a Catholic and an unbaptized person] can further aggravate these difficulties. (CCC 1634)

> But these differences can be lessened when the spouses share what they have received from their respective traditions and learn from each other how they fulfill their fidelity to Christ. (*USCCA* 289)

There is in some circles a major misconception. It is the belief that divorce actually exists in the Catholic Church. This is not true. While some marriages are annulled, this is distinct from divorce. What, then, is an annulment?

After investigation of a particular marriage, which might even seem to the whole world to be a true marriage in every way, the Church can determine that it was not so "from the very beginning." When this happens, the Church grants an annulment. That means that there never was a marriage "from the very beginning." If a marriage, for example, took place under grave external fear or under coercion, it could arguably be shown not to be a valid marriage. "For this reason (or for other reasons that render the marriage null and void), the Church, after an examination of the situation by the competent ecclesiastical tribunal, can declare the nullity of a marriage, that is, that the marriage never existed from the very beginning. In this case the contracting parties are free to marry, provided the natural obligations of a previous union are discharged" (CCC 1629). However, without an annulment, "the remarriage of persons divorced from a living, lawful spouse contravenes the plan and law of God as taught by Christ. They are not separated from the Church, but they cannot receive Eucharistic communion" (CCC 1665).

Marriage, moreover, must always be seen in the context of family life. As Pope Paul VI so beautifully taught: "The Christian family . . . can and should be called the domestic Church" (FC 21). The Church, indeed society, is built upon, grows from, depends upon this fundamental unit of the family. The fruitfulness of marriage involves parents not only in begetting children. Importantly, parents are the first teachers of their children in the ways of the faith. The family is a school of human virtue and love. "In our own time, in a world often alien and even hostile to faith, believing families are of primary importance as centers of living, radiant faith" (CCC 1656).

The great family of the Church is also open to the large number of single people, however, who, either by choice or circumstances, live in sincere and dedicated love of Christ and his Church. "No one is without a family in this world: the Church is a home and family for everyone" (CCC 1658).

Reflect

1. What do you know now about living your marriage vows that you didn't know when you first made them?

2. How have you experienced Christ's presence in your marriage?

3. What role does prayer play in your marriage and in your family?

4. How has the gift of children changed your experience of marriage?

Pray

A Prayer for Married Couples

Heavenly Father,
You have created man and woman
to be a reflection of your love for the world.
Bless our marriage and all married couples
that we might truly become
an image and likeness of you in the world.
May our love for one another share in your
    love
and fill us with a generous heart that is
    open to life.
When difficult times arise, surround us with
    your presence,
loving family, friends and parishioners
to give us the strength and grace we need.
Assure all married couples of your abiding
    presence
with us in good times and bad,
in sickness and in health
and for richer or for poorer.
May our lives be a witness to the world
of your loving care, faithful commitment
and persevering love for all people.
Amen.

—Archdiocese of Washington

References

References in the text to the *Catechism of the Catholic Church* are accompanied by the paragraph number, for example, (*CCC* 1066). References to the *United States Catholic Catechism for Adults* are given by the page number, for example, (*USCCA* 165).

Throughout the book you will also find references to the writings of John Paul II, Benedict XVI, and other popes, as well as to the documents of the Second Vatican Council. These documents are referred to by their English names and referenced by the abbreviation of their Latin title. For example, Pope Benedict XVI's encyclical *Saved by Hope* would be referenced *SS* for its Latin title *Spes Salvi*, followed by the paragraph number. While numerous editions of these documents exist, the quotations in this book are taken from the Vatican website: www.vatican.va. The site has an excellent search engine. For the most efficient search results, the Latin name of the document should be entered. A list of these can be found below. When quotations are taken from addresses by the Holy Father, these are noted by date. The full text of these addresses can be found by searching on the Vatican website by date.

Other sources quoted in this book are given by chapter in the order in which they appear.

Abbreviations

CCC Catechism of the Catholic Church. Vatican City: Libreria Editrice Vaticana, Second Edition, 1997.

USCCA United States Catholic Catechism for Adults. Washington, DC: U.S. Conference of Catholic Bishops Publishing, 2006.

CV Charity in Truth (Caritas in Veritate), Encyclical of Benedict XVI, 2009.

DD The Lord's Day (Dies Domini), Apostilic Letter of Pope John Paul II, 1998

DV On the Holy Spirit (Dominum et Vivificantem), Encyclical of Pope John Paul II, 1986.

EN On Evangelization in the Modern World (Evangelii Nuntiandi), Apostolic Exhortation of Pope Paul VI, 1975.

EV The Gospel of Life (Evangelium Vitae), Encyclical of John Paul II, 1995.

FC On the Christian Family in the Modern World (Familiaris Consortio), Apostolic Exhortation of John Paul II, 1981.

HV On Human Life (Humanae Vitae), Encyclical of Paul VI, 1968.

LG Light of the Nations (Lumen Gentium), Dogmatic Constitution on the Church, Second Vatican Council, 1964.

MD On the Dignity and Vocation of Women (Mulieris Dignitatem), Apostolic Letter of Pope John Paul II, 1988.

SC Sacrament of Love (Sacramentum Caritatis), Apostolic Exhortation of Pope Benedict XVI, 2007.

SS Saved by Hope (Spe Salvi), Encyclical of Pope Benedict XVI, 2007.

Chapter 1. Sacraments: Transforming Encounters with Christ

Gerald O'Collins and Mario Farrugia, *Catholicism* (New York: Oxford University Press, 2004), 234–235.

Pope Benedict XVI, *Jesus of Nazareth* (New York: Doubleday, 2007), 44, 353–354.

Chapter 2. Baptism: Gateway to the Christian Life

Pope Benedict XVI, 18.

Pope Benedict XVI, 23.

Pope Benedict XVI, 18.

Titled "The Hope of Salvation for Infants Who Die without Being Baptized," the study was originally commissioned by John Paul II. www.vatican .va / roman_curia / congregations / cfaith / cti_ documents / rc_con_cfaith_doc_20070419_un -baptised-infants_en.html

Gregory of Nazianzus, from the Office of Readings for the Feast of the Baptism of the Lord. *Oratio* 39 in *Sancta Lumina*, 14–16, 20; *PG* 36, 350–351, 354, 358–359.

Christian Initiation of Adults, 228.

Chapter 3. Confirmation: Be Sealed with the Gift of the Holy Spirit

O'Collins and Farrugia, 247.

Pope Benedict XVI, 22.

Francis Martin, *The Life-Changer* (Petersham, MA: St. Bede's Publications, 1998), 75–76.

Chapter 4. Eucharist: The Sacrament of Love

John Clarke, O.C.D., translator, *The Story of a Soul, The Autobiography of Saint Thérèse of Lisieux* (Washington, DC: ICS Publications, 1996), 77.

Karl Keating, *Catholicism and Fundamentalism* (San Francisco: Ignatius Press, 1988), 232–258.

Cardinal Angelo Comastri, Twentieth World Youth Day, 2005, Cologne, Germany.

Chapter 5. Eucharist: Ever Ancient, Ever New

Raniero Cantalamessa, *The Eucharist: Our Sanctification* (Collegeville, MN: Liturgical Press, 1993), 25–26.

Translation of *Ad Sacrosanctum Sacramentum* is from *The Aquinas Prayer Book* (Manchester, NH: Sophia Institute Press, 2000), 60–63.

Chapter 6. The Healing Sacrament of Penance

The decline has been well documented by the Center for Applied Research on the Apostolate (CARA) in *Sacraments Today: Belief and Practice Among U.S. Catholics*, April 2008. The study concluded in 2008 that 45 percent of Catholic adults never participate in the sacrament of Reconciliation and 30 percent participated less than once a year.

Quoted in James Martin, S.J., "Bless Me, Father," *America* (May 21, 2007), 14.

Donald Wuerl, quoted in Martin, 14.

Donald Wuerl, "Reflections on God's Mercy and Our Forgiveness," *The Catholic Standard* (January 31, 2008), 3.

John Paul II, "Address to the Bishops of Southern France, March 27, 1987," *Osservatore Romano* (May 11, 1987), 23.

Psalm 51 is from the Grail translation. *The Psalms* (Chicago: GIA Publications, 1963, 1986).

Chapter 7. Another Healing Sacrament: The Anointing of the Sick

"A Living Sacrifice" by John Gunstone is excerpted from *Fear Not, I Am With You* (Staten Island, NY: Alba House, 1990).

Chapter 8. Holy Orders: Apostolic Ministry

"The Brotherhood of Priests," Anonymous.

John O'Connor, "Holy Orders," *Catholic New York* (April 21, 1994).

John O'Connor, *On Being Catholic* (New York: St. Paul's / Alba House Publishers, 1994), 135.

"Spiritual Testament of Cardinal Pio Laghi," quoted by Pope Benedict XVI in his homily for the Funeral Mass of Cardinal Pio Laghi, January 13, 2009.

Chapter 9. Matrimony: It Takes Three

"Address of Benedict XVI to the American Bishops," April 16, 2008.

O'Collins and Farrugia, 292.

Msgr. Peter J. Vaghi is pastor of the Church of the Little Flower in Bethesda, Maryland, and a priest of the Archdiocese of Washington. Prior to his seminary studies at the North American College and the Gregorian University in Rome, he practiced law. He is chaplain of the John Carroll Society and the author of *The Faith We Profess: A Catholic Guide to the Apostles' Creed.*

Founded in 1865, Ave Maria Press,
a ministry of the Congregation of
Holy Cross, is a Catholic publishing
company that serves the spiritual and
formative needs of the Church and its
schools, institutions, and ministers;
Christian individuals and families; and
others seeking spiritual nourishment.

For a complete listing of titles from

Ave Maria Press

Sorin Books

Forest of Peace

Christian Classics

visit www.avemariapress.com

 ave maria press / Notre Dame, IN 46556
A Ministry of the Indiana Province of Holy Cross